Teachers for Tomorrow

Teachers for Tomorrow

Staff Development in the Community-Junior College

TERRY O'BANION

NATIONAL ADVISORY COUNCIL ON EDUCATION PRO-
FESSIONS DEVELOPMENT REPORT, originally submitted
to the President and the Congress of the United States
of America as "People for the People's College."

THE UNIVERSITY OF ARIZONA PRESS
Tucson, Arizona

THE NATIONAL ADVISORY COUNCIL ON EDUCATION PROFES-
SIONS DEVELOPMENT, established in 1967 by Public Law 90-35, was
charged with review of the Education Professions Development Act and all
other federal programs for training and developing educational personnel.
Council members, appointed by the President, are concerned with the various
levels of education from pre-school through graduate and professional training as well as with the full range of educational disciplines. While focusing on
the personnel needs of the community-junior college, in 1971 the Council
sketched the broad dimensions of this topic, commissioning Professor Terry
O'Banion to draft the report from which this volume was developed. O'Banion,
member of the faculty of the College of Education at the University of Illinois
since 1967, has been a consultant to community colleges in 40 states and
Canada. He has been Dean of Students at Santa Fe and Central Florida junior
colleges, and visiting professor at NDEA institutes for Junior College Counselors in Hawaii and at Florida State University. In the fall of 1972 he
became visiting professor at the University of California in Berkeley, major
U.S. center for junior college education.

MEMBERS OF THE COUNCIL

Mary W. Rieke (Chairman)
Member, House of Representatives
Oregon State Legislature

Larry J. Blake (Vice Chairman)
President, Flathead Valley Community·
   College
Kalispell, Montana

Jennie A. Caruso
Dean of Women
Maple Heights West Junior
   High School, Ohio

Jon William Clifton, B.D.
Louisville, Kentucky

Howard Coughlin
President, Office and Professional
   Employees International Union
New York City

George O. Cureton
Reading Consultant
East Orange, New Jersey

Rupert N. Evans
Professor, Vocational and Technical
   Education
University of Illinois

Hertzel Fishman
President, Sciences and Arts Camps, Inc.
New York City

Sidney Hook
Professor, Philosophy
New York University

Marvin D. Johnson
Vice President, University Relations
University of Arizona

Ted F. Martinez
Director, Student Union
University of New Mexico

Paul H. Masoner
Dean, School of Education
University of Pittsburgh

Janet Morgan
Guidance Director
South St. Paul High School, Minnesota

Lucius H. Pitts
President, Paine College
Augusta, Georgia

Joseph Young — Executive Director

Published by
THE UNIVERSITY OF ARIZONA PRESS
Manufactured in the U.S.A.

I. S. B. N.–0–8165–0391–5
L. C. No. 72–86973

Preface

The decade of the 1960s was the Decade of Quantity for the American community-junior college. The decade of the 1970s must be the Decade of Quality. If it is not, the community-junior college is in danger of becoming, by 1980, a mockery of our dream of "the people's college" and "democracy's college."

The quality of education in the community-junior college depends primarily on the quality of the staff. Community-junior colleges can enroll increasing numbers of students; they can develop a variety of educational programs; they can house these students and programs in attractive, modern facilities; but all these will avail little if their staffs are not highly competent and well prepared for the unique tasks assigned them by this new venture in American education.

Unfortunately, community-junior colleges and their supporters have misplaced their priorities. Administrators, state departments, federal officials, and professional associations have been enchanted by increased numbers — of students, of buildings, of colleges. There has been too little attention to the increased need for staff development. Unless the urgency and magnitude of this need is recognized immediately, and massive support is made available for creative and imaginative staff development programs, the full potential of the community-junior college will be unrealized and tens of thousands of Americans will have no opportunity for meaningful post high school education.

This report, prepared for the President's Advisory Council for Education Professions Development, describes the special characteristics of the community-junior college, its students, and its staff. It outlines major current efforts in preservice and inservice program planning and recommends programs designed to meet the various needs of staff. The scope of the report was restricted by certain unavoidable limitations of time and information.

A number of outstanding programs in universities and community-junior colleges exist for which no information was available. Information was particularly lacking on staff development programs for student personnel workers. It must be seen, therefore, as only a first step toward the development of specific programs with specific recommendations for funding by appropriate agencies.

The report focuses primarily on instructors, not only because more has been written on instructors, but because the need for them in program development is more acute.

Independent junior college and technical institute staff needs are not discussed separately. General staff development programs designed for public, comprehensive, community-junior colleges will require little or no modification to make them appropriate for these other institutions.

There are no specific funding recommendations; to have developed such recommendations would have required a thorough investigation of a massive array of complex programs and data. Such an investigation was beyond the scope of this project.

As it stands, this report should be useful in identifying needs and stimulating efforts for staff development. In particular it is vital that federal offices responsible for education will help foster the involvement of community-junior colleges, universities, and other agencies in making the 1970s indeed a Decade of Quality.

Acknowledgments

A number of people made significant contributions to this report. I am especially indebted to Robert Young, University of Illinois; Gregory Goodwin, Bakersfield College; and Gary James, Dallas Junior College District for their assistance in preparation of portions of the manuscript. Other people who have provided special assistance on projects connected with the report include James Buysse, Richard Colver, Larry Huffman, Terry Ludwig, Richard Mann, Larry Preo, Judy Riggs, and Michael Topper. Vincent DeLeers and Dorothy Bell provided invaluable editorial assistance. Sue Elman and Neva Wright provided excellent assistance in preparing the final manuscript.

A special word of thanks is due the approximately forty community-junior college leaders — administrators and instructors of community-junior colleges and university professors of community-junior college education — for the materials and ideas they so graciously shared. Their excellent response to our hurried call for assistance made the report possible.

The author is most appreciative also of the support provided by AAJC, Kellogg Foundation, ERIC and JCLP at the University of California at Los Angeles, The Center for Research and Development in Higher Education at Berkeley, and the Two-Year College Student Development Center, Albany. The University of Arizona Press should be recognized as well for its role in effecting publication.

TERRY O'BANION

Contents

Teachers for Tomorrow

Staff Development in the
Community-Junior College

1. The Growth and Development of the Community-Junior College

As the American public becomes increasingly aware of the community-junior college,* a number of paradoxes appear which limit public understanding and blur the identity of this newest and fastest growing segment in American higher education. Zealously proud of the excellence of their academic programs which propel students into four-year colleges and universities, community-junior colleges nonetheless broadcast their willingness to play an ever greater role in vocational training. Generally viewed as places where high school graduates can receive two more years of public education, it appears incongruous that half of community-junior college students are twenty-one years of age or older. Institutions once called "junior colleges" change their names to "community colleges" and often leave the public wondering why. Educated consumers, taught that "they get what they pay for," question how the community-junior colleges can claim both high quality and low cost. Community-junior colleges, attempting to be *all things to all people,* often find themselves in an "identity crisis" (Gleazer, 1968) since they are also *different things to different people.* Despite these paradoxes, however, the growth of community-junior colleges proceeds at a phenomenal rate.

In the fall of 1970, nearly 2,400,000 students were attending 1,070 community-junior colleges. (*Junior College Journal,* February, 1971). This was four times the number of community-junior college students in

---

*Many writers in the community-junior college movement use the terms "junior college" and "community college" interchangeably. The term "community-junior college" is used here to reflect the varied development and different types of community and junior colleges. It is descriptive of the community-junior college movement as a whole, but is not necessarily a term appropriate for any particular college.

1960, and nearly twice the number of community-junior colleges. According to the predictions of the Carnegie Commission on Higher Education, the United States will need to establish between 230 and 280 more community-junior colleges during the 1970s, and possibly between 400 and 450 if existing university branches and specialized two-year institutions do not develop more comprehensive programs. (Carnegie Commission on Higher Education, 1970). The widespread growth of community-junior colleges, despite public confusion about their precise identity, is an indication of the tremendous need for more educational opportunities beyond the high school.

People close to the movement and committed to its comprehensive goals, are aware that it is more than a hasty response to a frantic need. They know that the wide-ranging interests and aptitudes of young and adult men and women who enter through the "open door" have necessitated the multi-directional aims of the colleges. Further, they know that community-junior colleges have developed a tradition of attitudes and ideals, which has the potential to fuse their diversity of peoples and programs. This knowledge, however, makes the identity crisis all the more frustrating. For unless the people within the community-junior college movement can pass on to others their commitment to the traditional ideals and the unique goals of the movement, then these ideals and goals may fall victim to the centrifugal forces inherent in a multi-directional approach. Particularly critical is the matter of training new community-junior college workers — teachers, administrators, and student personnel workers — with the understandings and competencies which will enable them to work effectively with a diversified, comprehensive community-junior college. Of no less concern is the assisting of personnel already at work in community-junior colleges to develop further and apply better their own ideas and ideals.

Stages of Historical Development

As a relatively young and growing educational institution, the community-junior college has a natural tendency to promote interest in its future and its potential rather than in its history and its record of accomplishment. Indeed, compared to the university with centuries of history behind it, the community-junior college appears but an infant whose history can be summarized with mention of its founders and a chart of its linear growth since 1900. Looking forward, rather than backward, has permitted advocates of the community-junior college to maintain undismayed idealism while setting goals. At the same time it has hampered a realistic analysis of what the community-junior college is, and how it became what it is (Goodwin, 1971).

The community-junior college movement developed in stages. Each stage of growth displayed significantly different concepts concerning the fundamental role of the community-junior college in society. To understand the composition of ideals and programs in community-junior colleges today, it is necessary to become aware of the various stages and their related concepts.

The Formative Stage: Pre-World War I

At the beginning of the twentieth century, no public, two-year junior college is known to have existed. Yet the idea behind such an institution had been fully developed. This "junior college idea" was a product of both foreign influences and domestic needs.

The model of the German system of higher education was employed consistently by early advocates of the junior college — Henry Tappan, William Watts Folwell, William Rainey Harper, and David Starr Jordan, to mention only four. In particular these men were awed by the German university as a place for specialized study and research, free from the burden of elementary instruction and the care of adolescents. Tappan at Michigan, Folwell at Minnesota, Harper at Chicago, and Jordan at Stanford sought to direct their own institutions away from the English-Scottish-American tradition of liberal education and character-building and toward the German-type university. As a place to discard those functions not truly a part of the "higher learning," these university presidents advocated the development of an institution paralleling the German *Gymnasium*. The *Gymnasium* educated academic-minded youngsters in the liberal arts, taking them comfortably past adolescence to about their twentieth year. At that point the student could enter specialized study at the university or professional school or he could begin a career elsewhere. This convenient point of separation, when applied to the American system of higher education, came between the sophomore and junior year of the four-year college course. Since the first two years of college tended to general, survey-level courses, with specialization coming later, American educators were able to appreciate the logical divisions in the German system. Jordan was the first to label this "lower segment" of higher education the "junior college," and Harper was the first actually to establish such a junior college at the University of Chicago.

Historians of American higher education have chronicled the pervasive German influence in the thinking of university leaders at the turn of the century, but they have failed to probe deeply into the reasons why

Americans looked to Germany (Brubacher and Rudy, 1968; Rudolph, 1962; Veysey, 1965). Americans were no slavish imitators of European social inventions, and Germany in particular was suspected in the early twentieth century of undemocratic, villainous ways. Indeed, the admiration of American educators for the German system of education was generally mixed with disparaging remarks about the government and general character of the German nation (Goodwin, 1971). More attention needs to be paid to the domestic concerns of American educators which led them to select distant, autocratic Germany for a model of education.

American educators at the turn of the century, like other Americans, were caught up in the promise and peril of the industrial revolution. The promise of bountiful production and national power was made possible by science, technology, resources, and an efficient pool of labor. Ideally it was thought that man was evolving toward higher levels of morality — leaving behind him the slothful tendencies toward laziness, disorderliness, and inefficiency. The peril was that man might not rise soon enough to the level of efficiency necessary in the machine age — that inertia and tradition would prevent the masses from doing those things necessary for industrial success. Just as the machine offered a promise of perfection, man threatened the alternative of chaos. The controls of the family, the church, and the community were faltering. Unrestricted immigration was bringing hundreds of thousands of people to American shores whose race, religion, and culture were different. The life-styles of the immigrating aliens, as well as many less "production-minded" natives, appeared foreign to American dreams of an industrial utopia.

What was needed, educators urged, was an educational system geared to producing order, both in men and in society. Efficiency, in particular, became a key concept: it came to mean both the best way of doing things and the best way of being. All at the same time, it was a technique, a trait of character, and a moral value (Callahan, 1962). In this context, the junior college was promoted as a pedagogically efficient institution dedicated to the production of efficient men and women for society. It would mark the rational division point between general and specialized learning. It would shorten the number of years spent in pursuit of a bachelor's degree. (Most early advocates of the junior college assumed that it would complete a student's liberal education and grant the bachelor's degree.) It would produce both students capable of ascending to the university and workers prepared to take positions in society somewhere between the professions and the common laborers. The role of the junior college trained workers was generally defined socially rather than occupationally — they would be middle management in the ordering of society. They would be part of the bulwark against the masses backsliding toward inefficient and disorderly ways.

The desire for order and efficiency was a paramount factor in early efforts to establish junior colleges. William Rainey Harper, who divided the University of Chicago into junior and senior colleges in the late 1890s, was driven by a desire for efficiency not unlike his university's benefactor, John D. Rockefeller. A similar drive also characterized Folwell, Tappan, and Jordan. With this paramount objective, it is natural that the German system of education attracted their attention. More than any other system in the world, it reflected a concern for order and efficiency. Importing the basic structure of the German system and adapting it to a democratic society occupied the lives of many early twentieth century educators in American higher education. The same could be said for junior college advocates operating more within the framework of secondary education, such as California's Alexis F. Lange (Krug, 1969). Efforts to establish junior colleges were, in large part, only a single chapter in the broader attempts to make men and society more efficient.

At the end of World War I, a major study of American junior colleges reported the existence of many types — some connected to universities, some integrated with high schools, some extensions of private academies, and some normal schools for the training of teachers (McDowell, 1919). The public junior colleges, thirty-nine in number, were singled out by McDowell for their sizeable enrollments (larger than all other junior colleges, although there were twice as many such non-public institutions) and their accelerating growth rate. In every case, junior colleges were found to be closely tied to universities steeped with German-influenced university ideas. Emerging then from the peripheral vision of men whose focus was on the university, the identity of the junior college was blurred at its beginnings because of the lack of focus upon itself. McDowell concluded:

The junior college is in an experimental stage. We do not know what it should be, because we do not know what it is. Before we can see clearly what it is, we must know why it is. [McDowell, 1919.]

The Rise of Terminal Education: Between the Two World Wars

University men gave birth to the idea of the junior college, but its upbringing was entrusted to men primarily interested in secondary education. Leonard V. Koos, Walter C. Eells, and Doak S. Campbell were outstanding during the 1920s and 1930s among those who defined and propagated the junior college idea. All three accepted the important role of the junior college in preparing students for the university, but their main energies were devoted to the importance of "terminal education"— the proper preparation for the junior college student entering the world of work and the role of a citizen (Koos, 1925; Eells, 1931; Campbell, 1930).

Terminal education, as outlined by Koos, Eells, and Campbell, had a dual nature. It was, on one hand, vocational — to prepare students for semi-professional positions. On the other hand, terminal education was "citizenship training" — to produce in students the type of "social intelligence" which would make them law-abiding and hard-working persons. Of course, they all agreed that there was considerable overlap between being a good worker and a good citizen. All the same, Koos, Eells, and Campbell always distinguished between the training of the worker and the training of the citizen, and on balance they directed their efforts primarily toward the latter. Qualities of responsibility, loyalty, industriousness, efficiency, self-discipline, and patriotism were emphasized mostly for their salutary effect upon a citizen's community and larger society, although of course they were also promoted as educational outcomes valuable in any chosen occupation. In 1940, the American Association of Junior Colleges, aided by a grant from the General Education Board, launched a major study of junior college terminal education. Eells directed the study which underscored the need for terminal education and the shortcomings of junior colleges in providing it (Eells, 1941).

The greatest challenge to junior college educators during the 1920s and 1930s was one that has not since diminished. Despite their conviction that terminal education was necessary for a strong economy and an improved society, junior college students persisted in following the American dream of success, a dream that increasingly included a four-year baccalaureate degree. Terminal programs were developed in junior colleges which were "ideal" in the minds of their creators, but the educational consumers — the students — still selected university-parallel programs. Educators placed more and more reliance upon guidance workers to lead students to more "realistic" choices. Then as now, however, guidance workers achieved only minimal success in wakening students from the American dream.

More because of the open path to higher education than because of their success in terminal education, junior colleges multiplied in number during the decades between the world wars. Public junior colleges, soon to be called community colleges, increased in number from 39 in 1919 to 258 in 1940. Private junior colleges, generally committed to university-parallel programs,* increased in number to 317 during the same time. However, the private colleges enrolled less than one-third of the nation's junior college students (Eells, 1940).

---

*There are some important exceptions to this generalization. Private junior colleges such as Stephens College made important contributions to programs of terminal education by concentrating upon individual self-fulfillment.

The Search For General Education: World War II to Sputnik

After World War II, community-junior college leaders (here the term "community" began to creep into the phraseology) developed a preoccupation with general education. This was in part a continuation of the emphasis upon citizenship in terminal education, but it avoided the negative connotation that education actually terminated at any point in life. Like the old "terminal education," general education was heralded as the pedagogical path toward building good citizens, and thus good workers. Unlike the earlier concept of terminal education, however, general education was meant to apply to all community-junior college students, not only those in vocational or non-transfer programs. Two wars with Germany and the possibility of a war with the Soviet Union formed a backdrop of concern for rededicating the nation to a set of common, democratic ideals. Characteristically, the schools, including community-junior colleges, were expected to play the major role in strengthening and unifying American attitudes and ideals.

A major effort in defining and developing general education in the 1950s was sponsored by the Carnegie Foundation for the Advancement of Teaching. A fourteen-month study in California, the state at the forefront of community-junior college development at that time, involved over four thousand community-junior college participants. The study identified the following twelve goals of general education to help each student increase his competence:

(1) Exercising the privileges and responsibilities of democratic citizenship;
(2) Developing a set of sound moral and spiritual values by which he guides his life;
(3) Expressing his thoughts clearly in speaking and writing, and in reading and listening with understanding;
(4) Using the basic mathematical and mechanical skills necessary in everyday life;
(5) Using methods of critical thinking for the solution of problems and for the discrimination among values;
(6) Understanding his cultural heritage so that he may gain a perspective of his time and place in the world;
(7) Understanding his interaction with his biological and physical environment so that he may better adjust to and improve that environment;
(8) Maintaining good mental and physical health for himself, his family, and his community;
(9) Developing a balanced personal and social adjustment;
(10) Sharing in the development of a satisfactory home and family life;
(11) Achieving a satisfactory vocational adjustment; and
(12) Taking part in some form of satisfying creative activity and in appreciating the creative activities of others. [Johnson, 1952.]

Among other things, the California study concluded that appropriate general education could counteract a rising divorce rate, curb mental disorders, provide acceptable activities to fill the leisure-time needs of Americans, underscore common humanity, and be a step toward lasting peace. It was advocated also as the best form of vocational education since it was reported that many more workers, at a rate of nine to one, lost their jobs for "undesirable character traits" than for lacking technical skills.

While community-junior college leaders pondered general education, ever-growing numbers of students were flocking to their institutions. By 1955, nearly 700,000 students attended 581 public and private two-year colleges (Hillway, 1958). These students had strong interests in practical studies and sought paths to good careers but, like students of the previous generation, they were unwilling to enroll in programs which were not clearly transfer-oriented. And most general education programs designed around the goals stated above were not traditional and were often of dubious transfer value. These students were also aware that the bachelor's degree was becoming an increasingly visible marker on the paths toward better jobs. Good, transferable general education programs did not really have time to get established before the Soviet Sputnik gave rise to new and stronger educational forces.

The Commitment to Comprehensiveness: The Post-Sputnik Era

General education in the Soviet Union did not launch the first Sputnik into orbit. Realizing this, alarmed Americans insisted that their schools pay more attention to fostering technical and scientific expertise; life-adjustment programs lost their primacy and even became targets for critics anxious to assign blame for America's second rank in the space competition. The community-junior college, like other segments in the educational system, began to reappraise its role in the struggle for scientific supremacy. Emphasis upon skills took priority over any emphasis upon attitudes; programs to promote individual competencies took the spotlight away from programs to assure the acquisition of common knowledge and personal psychosocial development.

Rather than molding the diversity of community-junior college students into a common citizenry, the colleges began to tailor more diversified programs for their diversified student bodies. With the goal of each student developing those skills which would allow him to contribute his maximum productive capability to society, the ideal curriculum was seen as one which would assess varying potentials of students and train them accordingly. General education was not jettisoned in this trend toward specialization, but it was relegated a smaller and less respected slice of each student's program.

More and more, community-junior college leaders began to emphasize different specialized programs for various types of students. Vocational-technical programs were urged to prepare skilled workers for entry into the work force with a range of specialties, from waitresses to paramedical technicians. For students transferring to a four-year college or university, specialized courses in keeping with their declared majors were added so that they would lose neither time nor expertise, in comparison to "native" freshman and sophomore students at institutions where they were headed. Increasing numbers of adult students were offered programs to assist their career development, their home management, and their recreational interests. Students with records of low achievement were offered remedial programs. Guidance programs were expanded to help each student find his or her most efficient level of instruction as well as realistic vocational and life goals. None of these functions, of course, were new to community-junior colleges. Indeed, most of them could be traced back to the earliest of colleges. But never before were they so consistently and thoroughly meshed into a single concept of efficient individual development for the good of society. The central focus of the leaders was on the distribution of the right types of people into appropriate educational and vocational areas.

The broadening of community-junior college curricula within a commitment to comprehensiveness came during an era of unprecedented growth in the number of students attending these institutions. Economic and social forces were driving hundreds of thousands of young people toward higher education. The community-junior college, with a self-proclaimed reputation for the "open door," attracted the majority of these "new students" in higher education. Comprehensiveness became a necessity as well as a goal.

The Community-Junior College
As A Democratizing Institution

Throughout the various stages of growth in the community-junior college movement runs a common theme — the democratization of higher education. In many ways the development of community-junior colleges resembles the impact of the Morrill Acts of 1862 and 1890, which encouraged the development of land-grant colleges and universities. Both movements involved opening the doors of higher education even wider to attract new types of students. Both placed a great deal of emphasis upon new, practical programs of study — programs which faced a long uphill struggle to establish respectability in the halls of "higher learning." Both movements maintained unquestionably strong traditional curricular offerings alongside those that were more innovative, opting for comprehensive programs rather than separate technical or scientific schools.

Early land-grant colleges and present community-junior colleges even share common labels, such as "Democracy's Colleges" and "People's Colleges" (Ross, 1942). Edmund J. Gleazer, Jr. states: "The community college is the final link in the national chain of effort to democratize and universalize opportunity for college training" (Gleazer, 1971).

The democratizing influence of community-junior colleges does not end with providing a comprehensive curriculum and attracting new students into higher education. As a "community" institution, each community-junior college plays a unique role. Increasingly it is becoming the only social institution that cuts across racial, socioeconomic, and other distinct segments of the community in an attempt to reflect community needs. The studies of Dorothy Knoell demonstrate that community-junior colleges could do a better job of recruiting a fair proportion of students from lower-income families (Knoell, 1968, 1970), but the fact still remains that community-junior colleges, comparatively, are more representative of their communities than are most other educational and social institutions. As such, they can be democratic laboratories offering valuable experiences in community interaction and understanding.

The Community-Junior College
As A National Institution

Community-junior colleges generally have developed in keeping with the needs and the financial support of local areas. Some state governments have contributed substantial state support to the movement, generally without undermining the "community-centeredness" of the institutions. The federal government so far has been a less significant source of financial support, and only recently has an office for community colleges been established in the Bureau of Higher Education by Commissioner of Education Sidney P. Marland (Martin, 1971). Despite the "grass-roots" development of community-junior colleges, however, they have developed goals and programs which correlate highly with national goals. Dale Tillery has compared national goals and community college contributions as follows (Tillery, 1970):

NATIONAL GOALS	COMMUNITY COLLEGE CONTRIBUTIONS
EQUALITY OF OPPORTUNITY THROUGH EDUCATION	Open door to diverse programs at a low cost for youths and adults
NATIONAL ECONOMIC GROWTH AND WELL-BEING RESULTING FROM ADEQUATELY TRAINED MANPOWER	Well-planned and taught programs to provide for technical, managerial, and professional skills at several levels

EXPANDED OPPORTUNITIES FOR FULL INDIVIDUAL DEVELOPMENT	Opportunities for guided exploration of educational and career alternatives, and for relevant education
INCREASED EDUCATIONAL OPTIONS WITHIN COORDINATE SYSTEMS OF HIGHER EDUCATION	Comprehensive programs, including preparation, for students unprepared, unwilling, or financially unable to enter senior colleges at first matriculation
PROFESSIONAL OPPORTUNITIES FOR AMERICANS OF MINORITY BACKGROUND	Increasing opportunities as teachers, counselors, and administrators for Americans of diverse racial and ethnic backgrounds
ENHANCED QUALITY OF LIFE IN AN INCREASINGLY AFFLUENT SOCIETY	Community centers for cultural, intellectual, and personal renewal

To add to the list of paradoxes that began this chapter, the community-junior college is both a national and a community institution. Out of its deep-rooted and multifaceted history has emerged an institution as complex as it is comprehensive. In Chapter 2 will be presented a closer view of the characteristics and the curriculum of the community-junior college.

References

Brubacher, John S., and Rudy, Willis. *Higher Education in Transformation.* New York: Harper & Row, 1968.

Callahan, Raymond E. *Education and the Cult of Efficiency.* Chicago: University of Chicago Press, 1962.

Campbell, Doak S. *A Critical Study of the Stated Purposes of the Junior College.* Contribution to Education No. 70. Nashville: George Peabody College for Teachers, 1930.

Carnegie Commission on Higher Education. *The Open-Door Colleges: Policies for Community Colleges.* New York: McGraw-Hill Book Company, 1970.

Eells, Walter C. (ed.). *American Junior Colleges.* Washington, D.C.: American Council on Education, 1940.

————. *The Junior College.* Boston: Houghton Mifflin Company, 1931.

————. *Present Status of Junior College Terminal Education.* Terminal Education Monograph No. 2. Washington, D.C.: American Association of Junior Colleges, 1941.

Gleazer, Edmund J., Jr. "The Emerging Role of the Community Junior College." *Peabody Journal of Education,* XLVIII, No. 4 (July, 1971), 255–256.

————. *This is the Community College.* New York: Houghton Mifflin Company, 1968.

Goodwin, Gregory L. "The Historical Development of the Community-Junior College Ideology: An Analysis and Interpretation of the Writings of Selected Community-Junior College National Leaders from 1890 to 1970." Unpublished doctoral dissertation, University of Illinois at Urbana-Champaign, 1971.

Hillway, Tyrus. *The American Two-Year College.* New York: Harper & Brothers, 1958.

Johnson, B. Lamar. *General Education in Action.* Washington, D.C.: American Council on Education, 1952.

Knoell, Dorothy M. "Are Our Colleges Really Accessible to the Poor?" *Junior College Journal,* XXXIX (October, 1968), 9–11.

————. *People Who Need College: A Report on Students We Have Yet to Serve.* Washington, D.C.: American Association of Junior Colleges, 1970.

Koos, Leonard V. *The Junior College Movement.* Boston: Ginn and Company, 1925.

Krug, Edward A. *The Shaping of the American High School, 1890–1920.* Madison: University of Wisconsin Press, 1969.

McDowell, F. M. *The Junior College.* U.S. Bureau of Education Bulletin No. 35. Washington, D.C.: U.S. Government Printing Office, 1919.

Martin, Marie. "The Federal Government Behind the Open Door." *Peabody Journal of Education,* XLIII, No. 4 (July, 1971), 282–285.

Ross, Earle D. *Democracy's College: The Land-Grant Movement in the Formative Stage.* Ames: Iowa State University Press, 1942.

Rudolph, Frederick. *The American College and University.* New York: Vintage Books, 1962.

Tillery, Dale. "A College for Everyman." Berkeley: mimeographed, 1970.

Veysey, Laurence R. *The Emergence of the American University.* Chicago: University of Chicago Press, 1965.

2. Characteristics and Curriculum

The identity crisis of the community-junior college stems from unclear priorities rather than from any lack of distinguishing characteristics. Proponents of the movement generally agree that community-junior colleges are characterized by (1) open-door admission policies; (2) comprehensiveness; (3) community orientation; (4) emphasis upon teaching; (5) student centeredness; and (6) innovation.

Open-Door Admission Policies

At the very heart of the community-junior college movement, throughout all its historic stages, has been an unshakable belief in the educability of all people. While seeking acceptance as a *bona fide* segment of higher education, community-junior colleges have faced an ongoing struggle against the traditional academic view that "higher learning" is appropriate only for an intellectual elite. Dale Tillery, recommending "A College for Everyman," states:

... Segments of the academic community remain skeptical because traditional values and standards of higher education are, indeed, being challenged. Among the challenges are beliefs that all men are educable; that educational opportunities should be relevant to a wider range of human talents and abilities than those traditionally valued in higher education; that students with unsuccessful educational histories do achieve when given renewed opportunities to find themselves and to try new options. ... [Tillery, 1970.]

Community-junior college advocates have consistently argued that more, rather than fewer, Americans should enter the doors of institutions of higher education. How many more, however, is a question debated among community-junior college leaders themselves. A study by Huther (Huther, 1971) shows that a majority of public community-junior colleges require entering students to have a high school diploma or its equivalent. Further, nearly half the colleges with this entrance requirement also require that entering students be able to "profit by instruction" (See Table 2.1). The attitudes of community-junior college presidents, which were also assessed by Huther, were favorable toward admissions policies which would be more "open" than the existing policies (See Table 2.2).

[13]

TABLE 2.1

Catalogue Statements on Admissions Policy
For Full-Time Beginning Freshmen

Statements	N	Percent
Admit all whether high school graduates or not	44	7
Admit all who can profit from instruction whether high school graduates or not	243	39
Admit all with high school diplomas or the equivalent	202	33
Admit all with high school diplomas who can profit from instruction	122	20
No answer to this question	5	1
Total	616	100

(Huther, 1971, p. 26)

Since many colleges and universities across the nation have tightened their admissions policies by requiring better high school records and higher aptitude scores than ever before, the question of whether or not a community-junior college requires a high school diploma pales to insignificance. Much more important is the fact that community-junior college leaders have consistently and warmly embraced the idea that public education should exist beyond the high school for the many rather than for the few. The Educational Policies Commission of the National Education Association publicized a position in 1964 which struck a responsive chord in the community-junior college philosophy:

The goal of the universal education beyond the high school is no more utopian than the goal of full citizenship for all Americans, for the first is becoming prerequisite to the second. If a person is adjudged incapable of growth toward a free mind today, he has been adjudged incapable of the dignity of full citizenship in a free society. That is a judgment which no American conscious of his ideals and traditions can rightly make. [Educational Policies Commission, 1964, p. 360.]

TABLE 2.2

Admissions Policies Which Presidents Favor

Policy	N	Percent
Admit all whether high school graduates or not	62	10
Admit all who can profit from instruction whether high school graduates or not	332	54
Admit all with high school diplomas or the equivalent	91	15
Admit all with high school diplomas or the equivalent who can profit from instruction	131	21
Total	616	100

(Huther, 1971, p. 25)

Even if the doors of community-junior colleges were open to "every-man," with no entrance restrictions, that would not mean that the goal of universal education beyond the high school had been met. A necessary corollary to the open-door is *accessibility*. In actuality, community-junior college doors are accessible only to students within a commuting range. For students who have automobile transportation, this range might be from thirty to fifty miles; without automobile or public transportation some students might be limited to a commuting range of only a very few miles. There is a growing trend, especially in urban areas, to establish multi-campus community-junior college districts, rather than one giant campus, to make community-junior college programs more accessible to all residents of the community. In recognition of the important need to make "open door" colleges truly accessible, the Carnegie Commission on Higher Education, in its 1970 report, *The Open Door Colleges,* listed as the first of twelve major themes that community-junior colleges

. . . should be available, within commuting distance, to all persons throughout their lives, except in sparsely populated areas which should be served by residential colleges. This will require 230 to 280 new colleges by 1980. . . . Prospectively more than 95 percent of all Americans will be within commuting distance of a community college. [Carnegie Commission on Higher Education, 1970, p. 1.]

In addition to accessibility, the concept of the "open-door" college also implies *low cost to the student.* Many of the "new students" in higher education come from homes in the lower socioeconomic levels. Educational costs which might appear mild to more affluent college students can present major barriers to the "new students." Even in states such as California which charge no tuition to community-junior colleges, students face the costs of books and supplies, transportation, food while on campus, and institutional "fees." Students from low-income families must consider the loss of income that could come from a full-time job. Scholarships in community-junior colleges have perhaps alleviated this problem for the most promising students, but for community-junior colleges to continue to be open-door institutions they must maintain their policies of low student costs to attract the "new students" to American higher education.

Out of practical necessity, many community-junior colleges have been forced to install toll gates at the open door. Huther's study revealed that a majority of public community-junior colleges charged tuition of $200 or more during the 1968-1969 school year. Furthermore, Huther documented the rising number of colleges charging tuition, as well as the increasing amounts of tuition, since 1956 (See Table 2.3).

TABLE 2.3

Number and Percentage of Public Two-Year
Institutions Charging Tuition in
1956, 1960, and 1968

Tuition	1956		1960		1968	
	N	Percent	N	Percent	N	Percent
No tuition	112	36	121	35	133	18
$ 1- 99	77	25	39	12	91	13
100-199	86	28	118	35	196	27
200-299	17	6	34	10	156	21
300-399	4	1	11	3	90	12
400-499	0	0	16	5	60	8
500-up	11	4	0	0	8	1
Total	307	100	339	100	734	100

(Huther, 1971, p. 27)

Despite this ominous rise in cost to the student, community-junior colleges remain the greatest single hope for "breaking the access barriers" in American higher education for most low-income and minority-group American families (Medsker and Tillery, 1971).

While costs present the most obvious threat to the open-door policies of community-junior colleges, there exists a more subtle threat that the nation's commitment to universal higher education is slackening. Thornton combines the financial and ideological aspects of the problem of the open door as follows:

The open-door admission policy has been both the proudest claim and the knottiest dilemma of the community-junior college. At a time when enrollments are rising annually by hundreds of thousands of students, and when junior colleges are assuming an ever increasing share of freshmen and sophomore enrollments, is it possible to accept every student who requests admission? Is it possible to develop worthwhile college curriculums for all of them? Is it reasonable to accept students who are predestined to failure? Is it wise to conserve funds by denying admittance to applicants who fail to meet minimum intellectual or educational criteria? Does the American economy, or the "American dream," require that every high school graduate be provided opportunity for further education? [Thornton, 1966, p. 280.]

Even more disconcerting is the study of an open-door college by sociologist Burton R. Clark (Clark, 1960). Clark found that the community-junior college he studied acted primarily as a screening device for four-year colleges and universities. Students who came through the open door and who could not succeed in traditional college studies, Clark maintained, were systematically "cooled-out" by a process of "structured failure." If the community-junior college leads to pitfalls rather than the development of potentials, then indeed the open-door is a fraudulent claim.

There is a need to distinguish between an "open door" to the community-junior college and unrestricted admission to every program in the curriculum. Certain programs, such as nursing and electrical engineering, may be able to accept only a limited number of students because of the high cost of instruction and equipment. Such programs screen applicants to select those with the greatest potential for completing the program — those students who promise the highest return on the invesment. In some colleges, entry into "university-parallel programs" requires records of achievement and aptitude not unlike those required by universities.

There are, then, serious questions: how open is the door, and to where does it lead? Nevertheless, the concept of the open door remains a basic and viable ideal in the community-junior college movement and accords with national sentiments for increased opportunities in higher education. The President's Commission on Higher Education in 1947 advanced the then revolutionary idea that 49 percent of the American population could profit from two years of college instruction. The President's Committee on Education Beyond the High School in 1957 recommended that communities expecting substantial growth establish community-junior colleges for all high school graduates desirous of continuing their education. The President's Commission on National Goals went a step further in 1960 when it recommended that community-junior colleges be established within commuting distance of *all high school graduates in the nation,* except where a very sparse population would make this impractical. Most recently, the report of the President's Task Force on Higher Education has set the expansion of educational opportunity after high school as the nation's top "continuing priority," particularly the expansion of community-junior colleges (President's Task Force on Higher Education, 1970). Thus, the national commitment to the "open-door" is not shallow or transitory; it has evolved from a steady and persistent application of democratic ideals to higher education. It would indeed be a reversal of its democratic history if the community-junior college began to restrict enrollments rather than swinging its open door ever wider.

Comprehensiveness

One might question "How open is the open-door?" but it would have to be agreed that the door is open sufficiently at present to allow the entrance of a very diverse student body. Through that same door might walk the valedictorian of a high school class, a grandmother wanting to write poetry, a high school drop-out who never received a grade above a "D" and who cannot find steady employment, a businessman interested in improving his business and social skills, and a high potential flunk-out from the state university. All of these types of people, and many others besides, will generally find the door of a community-junior college open wide enough to let them in.

Naturally, it is one thing to accept a diversified student body and another thing to provide experiences and programs of sufficient breadth and depth to allow each student to pursue his or her educational goals. To be comprehensive, a community-junior college must, of course, offer a diversified curriculum. And most community-junior colleges do, as will be discussed more fully later in this chapter, offer transfer programs, career programs, general education programs, remedial-developmental programs, and continuing and adult education. But more than merely offering a potpourri of programs to a diversified student body, the comprehensiveness of community-junior colleges is a unifying value which permeates the spirit of the institution.

The comprehensiveness of community-junior colleges creates a democratic atmosphere within the colleges. Classes which attract students from a variety of programs offer opportunities for persons of varying backgrounds to learn about each other and from each other. Extra-curricular activities also produce a variety of group mixtures which help students appreciate the comprehensiveness of society at large. In this respect, the comprehensiveness of community-junior colleges can be considered an extension of the comprehensive high school, the democratic and educational merits of which James B. Conant lauded in *The American High School Today* (Conant, 1959). Residential patterns in many cases, however, as well as discriminatory policies in others, have made many high schools more comprehensive in programs offered than in students served. The community-junior college probably stands today as the best democratizer in the educational system, a distinction which rests in large part upon its commitment to comprehensiveness in the broadest sense.

Community Oriented

Most community-junior colleges can legitimately adopt the label of "community colleges" because they offer special interest courses for adults in the community at night, and because they offer special community services, such as public speakers, concerts, plays, group discussions, and the like. Some even offer health services and child care centers for community residents. Later in this chapter, the community-junior college service to adult and continuing education will be considered separately, even though often included under the rubric of community services. The community orientation which characterizes the strongest, most vital community-junior colleges in the nation, however, is a commitment which permeates all of its programs and which, *in toto,* is greater than the sum of its parts.

The actual label of "community college" did not emerge in the rhetoric of the community-junior college movement until after World War II, but leaders of the movement had designed the community-junior college to serve its community from its earliest days. Still, the role of consciously reflecting the community and participating in its development was not one that was clearly defined until the community-junior college movement was well under way. Only in recent years, as the community-junior college found itself in a unique position vis-à-vis the community, has the full potential of the institution as a community agent been apparent. As other levels of education and other institutions of society, including elementary schools, liberal arts colleges, service clubs, churches, etc., have become increasingly geographically restricted, socioeconomically restricted, or both, the community-junior college has become more unique as an institution of, by, and for the entire community. Only a generation or two ago, most communities had one park, one theater, one ball team and ball park, and one city square. This oneness helped to promote community-mindedness. Today there are few such opportunities for most communities, physically or symbolically, to come together. Community-junior colleges, with the broadest application of community-mindedness, can provide such opportunities.

One of the first community-junior college leaders to emphasize the community role of community-junior colleges was Jesse P. Bogue. He described this role in the broadcast dimensions of community life:

The philosophy of the community college for America takes on something of the flavor of the folk-schools of Scandinavian countries and the country colleges in England. Their primary purpose is to enrich the quality of community living in order to enable the people to enjoy the fruits of their labors. The community college does not exist for the sake of the university, nor to produce efficient workers as tools in an industrialized society, nor further, to keep money in local communities that might be spent by students in other college centers. Increasing emphasis is being placed on general education in the social sciences and the humanities as an indispensable part of the community college program for all students, regardless of their vocational aims. Hereby, an enriched and enlarged personality may be gained by means of and within the framework of democratic government. This is the goal. [Bogue, 1948, p. 292.]

The community role of a community-junior college, however, goes even beyond the lofty goals of strengthening bonds and offering services. Ideally, it is also an agent for change, actively involved in stimulating community development. There is, of course, a difficult balance to strike between reflecting community attitudes and interests on the one hand, and leading the community toward beneficial changes, some of which might upset the status quo. The community-junior college must try to do both — its effectiveness as a change agent stems from its efforts as a part of the community, not as an alien force. The Executive Secretary of the American Association of Junior Colleges thinks that the community-junior college will increase its community effectiveness as a change agent: "I can say . . . without equivocation that the community junior college will become an increasingly more viable instrument of social and cultural change" (Gleazer, 1971, p. 255).

Emphasis Upon Teaching

Unlike four-year colleges and universities which reward highly scholarly research and professional consulting, community-junior colleges generally expect their staffs to devote themselves to the singular task of teaching. Arthur M. Cohen, director of the Junior College Teacher Preparation Program at the University of California, Los Angeles, states:

The scholar-researcher is not sought by the junior college and is rarely found therein. The institution sets its face sternly against the practice of extensive academic research and paid consultation with industry and public agencies — two activities central to scholarly life at the major universities. Junior college teachers are told they will be judged on the basis of their teaching. Coupled with the initial role-choice of the new teacher, the organizational climate exerts a force for "teaching" too powerful, in most instances, for a single individual to overcome, no matter how much he wishes to be considered primarily as a member of an academic field. [Cohen, 1969, p. 97.]

Thus, community-junior colleges seek not communities of scholars, but rather communities of learners. Approximately two-thirds of community-junior college faculty members hold master's degrees, and approximately ten percent hold doctoral degrees (Thornton, 1966; Reynolds, 1969). Yet even with these degrees, community-junior college teachers find that they too must be part of the "learning community"; the community-junior college emphasis upon teaching encourages them to find new ways to teach their subjects and to learn more about the students who fill their classrooms (Garrison, 1967).

Community-junior college teachers come from a variety of backgrounds. One national study determined that thirty percent of new community-junior college instructors had previously been high school teachers, twenty-four percent had entered from graduate schools, and eleven percent had come from business occupations, leaving an "other" category of nearly eighteen percent (Maul, 1965).

The common denominator among these diverse instructor types is their attraction to a college which clearly and proudly characterizes itself as a teaching institution. Refugees from universities who protest high rewards for research and not for teaching, and ex-businessmen who seek to share what they have learned, can find a common bond in their interest in conducting relevant, stimulating classes.

Community-junior college instructors find teaching more than a full-time job. The average instructor spends fourteen to eighteen hours a week in the classroom. Approximately the same amount of time is spent each week preparing for classes and evaluating the work of the students. Another similar time block is used for individual conferences, meetings, assisting student activities, and the like. Total hour commitments per week generally average 45 to 55 hours (Garrison, 1967; Hillway, 1958). Even with this major commitment, Garrison, reporting on a major study of community-junior college faculties, discovered that the major problem faced by faculty members was a shortage of time to spend on teaching:

There is not enough time, the teachers said, to keep up in my own field; to develop innovations or new methods in my own teaching; to do a proper job with individual students; to investigate what other junior colleges are doing; to study for myself; to discuss educational matters with my fellow-teachers; even, more often than I like to think, to do a decent job of preparation for my classes; to refresh myself, even occasionally, by brief association with some of my colleagues in my own discipline, whether at conventions, special regional meetings, or whatever; or function effectively on faculty committees; to help in advising student organizations. [Garrison, 1967.]

The emphasis upon teaching in community-junior colleges, however, is not so overpowering that it can counteract completely the appeal of the academic ideal — the university emphasis upon scholarly research and expertise in one's academic discipline. Most community-junior college instructors have been trained in universities and have drunk deeply from the chalice of academe; they enter their institutions with academic biases which seem to conflict abruptly with their responsibility for teaching the common man. Medsker reported that nearly half the community-junior college instructors, based on a national sampling, would prefer to be employed at a four-year college or university (Medsker, 1960). Perhaps this response reflects in part the higher social status granted to instructors at a "higher" education level, but there is reason to believe that much of it reflects kindred aptitudes and interests with more "academic" institutions. Medsker found in the same study that 28 percent of the community-junior college instructors sampled thought it "not important" to offer remedial high school level courses at their institutions. Twenty percent of the instructors thought it "not important" for community-junior colleges to offer vocational or in-service courses for adults. Furthermore, 44 percent of the faculty members felt that entrance standards for their institutions were too low, a significant minority for a staff reportedly committed to the concept of the "open door."

The present oversupply of job-seekers with master's degrees and doctorates presents both a danger and an opportunity to community-junior colleges seeking to strengthen their instructional programs. The danger is that a greater number of Ph.D.'s, trained in research methodology, will enter community-junior college teaching and bring with them academic biases along with their academic expertise. The tendency for persons and institutions in higher education to emulate the model above in the academic hierarchy has been described by Thornton:

> The problem lies in ensuring that the faculty will exert its influence toward the realization of the full set of junior college tasks, rather than seeking to shape the institution in the image of the university. Land-grant colleges have become great state universities, to the point where they are embarrassed by the original purpose. Normal schools have become great state universities, without improving their competence or pride in the preparation of teachers for the public schools. Can junior college faculties resist this emulative drive and push on toward their own excellence? Or will it be necessary in another quarter century to establish anew an institution to perform the tasks that by then the junior college will have abandoned? [Thornton, 1966. p. 286.]

Behind the present surplus of qualified academicians, which according to most predictions will only be temporary, lies an advantage as well as a pitfall for community-junior colleges. It is now possible for community-junior colleges to pick and choose qualified instructors from an ample list of candidates; they can screen staff for appropriate attitudes and skills which really underlie good community-junior college teaching. Many community-junior college leaders believe that the percentage of Ph.D.'s teaching in community-junior colleges will *not* appreciably increase despite the present surplus; they assert instead that community-junior colleges will continue to draw from the pool of candidates committed to the open-door concept and skilled in teaching (Gleazer, 1971-A; Medsker and Tillery, 1971). With these developments, some colleges and universities are making efforts to make their degree holders more employable. Special programs for prospective teachers interested in community-junior colleges in particular, with emphasis upon the history, philosophy, and characteristics of that segment of higher education and also upon teaching skills, are more likely to lead to jobs than is the traditional academic degree (Fordyce, 1971). New degrees, such as the Master of Philosophy and the Doctor of Arts, which include teaching internships and interdisciplinary course patterns, may contribute to the effectiveness of teaching in community-junior colleges (Carnegie Commission on Higher Education, 1971).

If there is indeed a diminution of the problem of finding new staff members for burgeoning community-junior colleges, a new emphasis is likely to develop on in-service training programs. To be a "community of learning" in a real sense, community-junior colleges are realizing the importance of assisting their own staffs to develop their talents and potentials. The Florida legislature recently approved "three percent money" (three percent of the state's total community-junior college budget) to be used specifically for faculty and program development beyond existing development programs (Wetzler, 1970). At the University of California, Berkeley, Chester H. Case is assisting community-junior college instructors to improve their teaching techniques through video-taping and peer-feedback sessions (Case, 1971). At the heart of all developing preservice and inservice programs for the training of community-junior college instructors is *teaching*. If these programs are successful, then the community-junior college will indeed remain a *teaching* institution.

Student-Centered

The community-junior college emphasis upon teaching has a natural corollary — a pressing concern with the classroom learner. Student-centeredness is the hallmark of good classroom teaching. But the community-junior college has earned a reputation for student centeredness that extends beyond a concern for the student as a classroom learner. The community-junior college seeks the full development of the human potential. A basic assumption behind the community-junior college movement has been expressed by Collins and Collins as follows:

The Purpose Of Education Is To Help Each Man Experience More Fully, Live More Broadly, Perceive More Keenly, Feel More Deeply, To Pursue The Happiness of His Own Self-fulfillment and to Gain the Wisdom To See That This Is Inextricably Tied To The General Welfare. [Collins and Collins, 1966, p. 7.]

Soul-searching questions of identity and self-fulfillment are not separate from questions of program choice and career orientation. Students often enter through the "open door" seeking new roads to success, for opportunities to discover their own self potentials and to define their life goals. This search may be reflected in indecision about a program of study, or about particular courses. Community-junior colleges have attempted to provide topgrade professional assistance for students facing such decisions. This commitment has made student personnel programs in community-junior colleges more than just an adjunct to the curriculum; the executive director of the American Association of Junior Colleges has described student personnel work as "a senior partner in the junior college" (Gleazer, 1967.).

Traditionally, student personnel workers in community-junior colleges have operated on a service model; that is, they offered counseling, financial aids, health services, college orientation, and other services which would foster students' success in a college. A new type of student personnel worker might be labeled a "human development facilitator" (O'Banion, 1971), one who is less service-oriented and more individual-oriented. Through devices such as human development seminars, peer counseling, student-faculty communications laboratories, and self-improvement contracts, the human development facilitator can assist students to "experience more fully, live more broadly, perceive more keenly, and to feel more deeply . . ."

Jane Matson, a national authority on student personnel work in community-junior colleges, has predicted that student personnel workers will increasingly offer their services to teachers and administrators, rather than limiting their services to students. Matson maintains:

Student personnel staff are being provided opportunities to serve as resource consultants to faculty and administrators in such areas as curriculum design and development, classroom learning problems, evaluation and follow-up. The potential for the use of student personnel staff in this new role is not yet fully realized, but it is a practice which appears to offer promise, especially in efforts to serve the new students. [Matson, 1971, p. 279.]

Student personnel work, unfortunately, is recognized more in the rhetoric of the community-junior college movement than it is in actuality. A study by the National Committee for Appraisal and Development of Junior College Student Personnel Programs of twenty-one basic student personnel services in 1965 found that "when measured against criteria of scope and effectiveness, student personnel programs in community junior colleges are woefully inadequate (National Committee for Appraisal and Development of Junior College Student Personnel Programs "Foreword"). By its own standards, the role of the community-junior college in student personnel work is deficient. Compared to most other colleges and universities, however, this function of community-junior colleges stands out as a major strong point.

Innovation

Community-junior colleges are relatively new educational institutions. With a minimum of traditional limitations, they should be fertile grounds for innovation. New community-junior colleges are opening at a rapid rate, and energetic community-junior college leaders with new visions and innovative approaches rapidly find a variety of positions calling for their talents. Community-junior colleges seek to introduce "new students" to "new programs" in higher education; thus, it is not surprising that they put a premium on innovation.

At least it seems reasonable that community-junior colleges would have an inside track on innovation. So thought B. Lamar Johnson in 1963 when he made an exploratory national survey of community-junior college teaching innovations. His report was entitled — *Islands of Innovation* — indicating that innovation was not as widespread as it might have been. Johnson stated:

The general picture revealed in the survey is one of significantly less experimentation than would be expected, or certainly hoped for, in an institution which is often referred to as "the most dynamic unit in American education." [Johnson, 1964, p. 3.]

More recently, Johnson completed an eighteen-month study of community-junior college innovations — and reported his findings under an encouraging title: *Islands of Innovation Expanding*. Visiting community-junior colleges across the country, Johnson discovered a volumeful of innovations, including cooperative work study education, programmed instruction, audio-tutorial teaching, TV classes, games and other simulation in teaching, and so forth. Yet, despite an abundance of innovations, Johnson stated:

Although change has occurred in education, it has failed to keep pace with other developments in society. The necessity for change is, however, currently recognized, and innovation has become *avant-garde* in American education. Tomorrow's education is, in a very real sense, being conditioned and fashioned by developments now taking place in our schools and colleges. [Johnson, 1969, p. 315.]

Innovations in college may indeed have far to go, but community-junior colleges have been willing to start the journey. Consortiums such as the League for Innovation and GT-70 have launched collective efforts on behalf of innovation. Community-junior college instructors are fully aware that the "new students" in American higher education are unlikely to respond enthusiastically to traditional programs which employ instructional tactics that have failed all along to serve their purposes. People committed to innovation find a natural home in community-junior colleges.

The importance of such reform-minded educators was highlighted in the First Annual Report of the National Advisory Council on Education Professions Development:

There is a growing appreciation of how central education is to the realization of individual and national aspirations. The quality of that education, therefore, becomes increasingly critical. We are now in the beginning stages of a substantial undertaking to reform and improve American education. Ultimate success in this will turn not only on dollars, and facilities, and organizational arrangements — but especially on people. To focus on the people of education, then, is to focus on the heart matter of educational reform. [National Advisory Council on Education Professions Development, 1968, p. 3.]

The drawbacks to innovation in community-junior colleges are the bonds of tradition and the difficulties of breaking new educational ground. Often, the spirit is willing but the practical knowhow is missing. To maintain and to encourage innovation in community-junior colleges, it is becoming increasingly important to concentrate efforts upon encouraging innovative training programs for potential community-junior college personnel.

The Community-Junior College Curriculum

There is no common curricular design which applies to all community-junior colleges. Generally speaking, however, community-junior college programs fall into five categories: (1) transfer programs; (2) career programs, (3) general education; (4) remedial-developmental programs; and (5) continuing and adult education.

Transfer Programs

Every community-junior college has programs permitting students to transfer to four-year colleges and universities. This traditional function was embedded in community-junior colleges by their earliest founders, men such as Tappan, Folwell, Harper, and Jordan. Not only are transfer programs first traditionally, but often, since they are relatively inexpensive, they are the first programs established by new community-junior colleges, ahead of many of the career programs, and having instructors and students readily available to man the programs.

Duplicating transfer or university-parallel programs in community-junior colleges is easily justified. Four-year colleges and universities can well afford relief from the vast numbers of students applying for admission. More importantly, students with limited financial resources, many of whom plan extended and expensive future graduate programs or professional programs or both, are given the opportunity to complete the first two years of their college program while living more economically at home. Some students are not ready at age eighteen to assert the independence and self-direction necessary for their survival at a distant university. In addition, transfer programs in community-junior colleges often present second chances to students with undistinguished high school records, and to university dropouts, qualified students who were not ready to encounter the university when they did.

Approximately one-third of all fulltime community-junior college students do transfer to four-year colleges and universities. Seventy-five to 80 percent of this number achieve their degree objective within four years after transfer (Knoell and Medsker, 1965). While suffering initial "transfer shock" which lowers most transfer students' grade-point averages a quarter of a grade point, they generally accomplish their baccalaureate programs with records almost indistinguishable from "native" four-year college and university students. Although the dropout rate is higher among transfer students than "native" students, the community-junior colleges can boast of remarkable success in placing their transfer students.

The success of transfer programs paradoxically has created one of the major problems confronting community-junior colleges. While committed to a comprehensive curriculum to meet the differing needs of its diversified student body, many community-junior colleges have found that the appeal of transfer programs actually detours many students away from non-transfer programs more appropriate to their interests and skills. The recognized status of academic transfer programs seems to influence students, faculty, and administrators. Medsker's findings on the university orientation of many faculty have already been mentioned. Kimball surveyed administrator and faculty attitudes in Michigan community-junior colleges and disclosed that 82 percent of his respondents believed that the college-transfer segment of the curriculum was of greater importance than any other part (Kimball, 1960).

Students show their preference for transfer programs by enrolling in them in the ratio of two to one over other college programs. In other words, while approximately one-third of community-junior college students actually transfer, nearly two-thirds of them enroll in "university parallel" programs. Despite extensive efforts in the way of counseling and guidance, many students launch upon a transfer program which leads them neither to transfer nor to program-related employment. Some critics maintain that community-junior colleges really act as screening devices for higher educational levels, permitting able students to transfer and purposely "cooling out" the rest through a system of structured failure so that they will accept a lower position in society (Clark, 1960). On the other hand, some critics blame community-junior colleges for accentuating transfer programs and failing to guide students with a firm hand into those programs commensurate with their abilities (Blocker, Plummer, and Richardson. 1965). Analyses differ, but most agree that the discrepancy between the number of community-junior college students that aspire to transfer and the number that actually transfer stands as a major problem.

Career Programs

Separating community-junior college programs into transfer and career categories can be misleading. Most transfer programs have clear career orientations — business, teaching, engineering, etc. Some community-junior college writers try to avoid this categorization altogether, speaking of general, liberal, preprofessional, and occupational studies (Schultz, 1971), or general, preparatory, and vocational education (Reynolds, 1969). Indeed, it is often difficult for community-junior colleges themselves to specify which programs are transferable and which are not, since many four-year colleges and universities make their own determination on such matters. Despite the confusion, however, most community-junior colleges do offer programs clearly designed to lead to career entry at the conclusion of the program.

The range of career-entry positions for which community-junior colleges prepare students is very wide. A sampling of career programs has been categorized by Harris as follows:

1. *Business-related occupations*

   Accounting — bookkeeping
   Advertising layout
   Business data processing
   Business data programming
   Buying — purchasing
   Credit and collections
   Insurance

   Real estate
   Salesmanship
   Secretary — many options
   Stenographer
   Store management
   Typist clerk

2. *Health-related occupations*

   Certified (medical) laboratory
     assistant
   Dental hygienist
   Dental laboratory technician
   Dental office assistant
   Histologic technician
   Hospital aide
   Inhalation therapy technician
   Medical laboratory technician

   Medical office assistant
   Mental health worker
   Practical (vocational) nurse
   Prosthetic technician
   Psychiatric aide
   Radioisotope technician
   Registered nurse (A.D.N. or
     diploma)
   X-ray technician

3. *Research-related occupations*

   Ballistics technician
   Biological technician
   Biophysical technician
   Chemical technician
   Geophysical technician
   Hydrographic technician

   Mathematics aide
   Metallurgical technician
   Meteorological technician
   Oceanographic technician
   Physics research technician
   Spectroscopy technician

4. *Engineering-Industry-related occupations*

    A. Related to mechanical occupations

Aerospace technician	Industrial technician
Air conditioning/refrigeration technician	Inspector
	Machine operator
Automotive mechanic	Machinist
Automotive technician	Materials test technician
Diesel mechanic	Operating "engineer"
Draftsman (several options)	Plant foreman
Foundry technician	Plant maintenance mechanic
Heavy equipment mechanic	Quality control technician
Hydraulics technician	Tool and die technician

    B. Related to electrical/electronic occupations

Aerospace technician	Hydroelectric plant operator
Electric motor repairman	Instrumentation technician
Electrical power technician	Lineman (electric power)
Electronic technician	Missile technician
Options:	Steam plant operator
Communications, Computer,	Telephone installer
Industrial electronics, Radio,	Wireman
Television, Telephone,	
Microwave	

    C. Related to contract construction and civil engineering occupations

Architectural draftsman	Concrete test technician
Building construction supervisor	Estimator
Building construction technician	Heavy equipment operator
Building inspector	Materials test technician
Building trades journeyman	Sanitation technician
(several options)	Surveyor

    D. Miscellaneous technical and skilled occupations in industry

Ceramics technician	Petroleum technician
Chemical technician	Radioisotope technician
Engineering technician	Sales "engineering"
Nuclear power technician	Technical illustrator
Optical technician	Technical writer

5. *Public-Service and Personal-Service occupations*

Audiovisual technician	Law enforcement occupations
Baker	Mosquito abatement technician
Barber	Motion picture operator
Cafeteria manager	Nursery school operator
Chef (Cook)	Regional planning technician
Cleaning and pressing operator	Sanitation technician
Cosmetician	Security patrolman
Dining-room hostess	Service station attendant
Environmental control technician	Social worker aide
Fireman (fire department)	Teacher aide
Fish and wildlife technician	Tour guide
Forestry technician	Waiter/waitress
Hotel and restaurant occupations	

6. *Agricultural Occupations*

Agri-business jobs, n.e.c.	Feed mill operator
Agricultural research technician	Food processing technician
Crop-duster (aviator)	Frozen food plant operator
Farm equipment repairman	Irrigation specialist
Farm equipment salesman	Landscape designer
Farm supplies salesman	Nursery operator
Farmer (owner or manager)	Soils technician

[Harris, 1967, pp. 251–253.]

Career programs are receiving increasing emphasis in community-junior colleges. Although they must compete with what Blocker, Plummer and Richardson call the "halo effect" of transfer programs, they appear on the way toward achieving a sanctification of their own. Federal aid has tended to encourage this aspect of community-junior college curriculums (Martin, 1971). Schultz reports that the growth of community-junior college occupational programs during recent years "has been nothing short of phenomenal." Schultz studied 20 institutions, two randomly selected from each of 10 various states, and discovered marked changes over a twelve year period:

Occupational Programs	*1958–59*	*1970–71*
Average number of programs offered	9.2	36.4
Least number offered by an institution	2	9
Largest number offered by an institution	23	80

[Schultz, 1971, p. 265.]

To break the tradition and status-granting hold of college transfer programs upon community-junior college students, good career programs are necessary. Furthermore, by stressing career *entry* and not a total life commitment, community-junior colleges can avoid the implication that a career-orientated program necessarily prohibits other options later in life. According to the Carnegie Commission on Higher Education:

Young people should . . . be given more options (a) in lieu of formal college, (b) to defer college attendance, (c) to step out from college to get service and work experience, and (d) to change directions while in college. [Carnegie Commission on Higher Education, 1971, p. 1.]

If community-junior colleges can add alternatives to the either-or choice between transfer and career programs, they will take a major step indeed in breaking the academically biased lockstep toward higher education.

General Education

While modern trends in community-junior college education have been concerned primarily with the differences among students, focusing upon diversified programs to meet those differences, there remains in community-junior college ideals and programs a strong commitment to general education. All college students, regardless of diversity, will be citizens and thus will need basic understandings of the democratic way of life. All will have to relate with their fellowman as well as confront serious questions concerning their own values. The types of general education goals mentioned in Chapter 1 continue to be valid community-junior college aims.

In making the "Case for the Community College," Collins and Collins underscored the importance of general education in the community-junior college:

[There is an] essential difference between the value perception of the comprehensive community college and that of the technical institute. The latter works toward producing a well-honed, efficient, productive cog who will fit neatly into the economy and who will find his satisfactions in the rewards of the economy. The comprehensive public community college makes the rejoinder that if economic productivity were the only aim, then the stockholders to whom the profit will accrue should pay for the training of the worker, just as they pay for the machine which he will operate. Education is an obligation of the total society because it is the total man, not just the economic man, who, one by one, makes up the membership of that society. It is this unequivocal insistence that no part should dominate the whole, that a man is a man not just a unit of production, which lies behind the resistance of many curriculum committees to establish certificate programs in vocational specialties, and which explains the frequent 1:1 ratio of general to specialty education written into the graduation requirements. This last observation applies as much to the transfer student as to the technical-vocational student. If the associate in arts or associate in science degree calls for a minimum of sixty semester units, then no more than thirty should be in a specialty field whether that specialty be pre-professional chemistry or pre-vocational electronics. In either case the remaining thirty units should be devoted to those common elements which experience has demonstrated to be essential to preparation for manhood, for fulfillment of potential, for self-actualization. [Collins and Collins, 1966, pp. 27–28.]

Not all community-junior colleges go as far as following the Collins' suggestion that half of a student's program be devoted to general education. More commonly, one-third or less of a student's program is specifically so labeled. Even then, general education is often acquired piecemeal, with each student selecting a miscellaneous group of courses which satisfy some "field" requirement. More often than not, these courses are not geared specifically to general education but rather serve as introductions to academic desciplines. Attacking myths about community-junior college education, Arthur Cohen charges that "the one that perpetuates the fiction that junior colleges offer a liberal general education to their students" is "the cruelest myth of all" (Cohen, 1969, p. 83).

General education has taken on a variety of meanings over the years (Brubacher, 1965). In some colleges it is offered as a separate program, distinct from both transfer and career programs. In this regard it is often a euphemism for a low-level, non-transfer developmental program. Most community-junior colleges offer general education as a component part of specialized programs, whether they be transfer, career, or developmental. Within this framework there is a variety of approaches, from general education courses geared to each special program to a college-wide general education sequence which purposely brings together in classes a cross section of the student population. The latter approach presents a good opportunity for students to learn about and from each other. Notable programs of this type are in operation: Santa Fe Community College in Florida has a core general education program for all of its students, including BE-100, a course on The Individual in a Changing Environment. Among other things, this course helps students to integrate individual experiences and larger values; a democratic group setting facilitates the process (O'Banion, 1971).

Remedial-Developmental Programs

As the door of the community-junior college opens ever progressively wider, it is obvious that through it will come an increasing number of students with records of low achievement and without the developed skills which would allow them to perform satisfactorily in most college classrooms. It is estimated that 30 to 50 per cent of the community-junior college students are in need of developing basic skills (Medsker and Tillery, 1971). If the open-door is to be left open to these low achievers, as most community-junior colleges maintain that it should, then remedial-developmental programs must be provided to assist such students to make up for lost development. O'Banion states:

The junior college has made a commitment to the undereducated of this country that no other institution of higher education has ever dared make. It is a bold commitment and a commitment that reflects the democratic-humanitarian philosophy upon which the junior college rests. If the junior college can succeed in providing meaningful educational experiences for those who have known only failure, then no one will doubt its claim of uniqueness. [O'Banion, 1969, p. 9.]

While most community-junior colleges do have some sort of remedial program, it too often receives minimal support and shows discouraging results (Roueche, 1968). Johnson found a few encouraging signs of promising developmental programs in his survey of community-junior college innovations, but he concluded that "sound and imaginative plans for teaching vast numbers of low-achieving students are greatly needed" (Johnson, 1969, p. 206). There are some community-junior college leaders who caution against making too great a commitment to educating the lower levels of mental abilities.

The public two-year college cannot simultaneously be a quality educational institution and a custodial institution. As society generates larger numbers of individuals who cannot meet minimum levels of competence, specialized institutions must be created to deal with the problem. These may be combinations of work camps and schools, or they may be organized in other patterns. The point is that there are some limitations to the ability of any one organization to handle all social problems. These limitations are apparent in comprehensive urban high schools, where individuals of very low mental ability are put with those of normal and higher ability. [Blocker, Plummer, and Richardson, 1965, pp. 273–274.]

Whether because of such an acceptance of limitations, or because of a lack of resources, or because of poor techniques, or because of a combination of all of these, community-junior colleges have not, at any rate, satisfactorily performed this "salvaging function." The programs are often staffed by new teachers without special training who see these low-level classes as a step on the ladder to transfer courses. What are called developmental courses too often merely repeat the same tactics and content that the student was exposed to, with little effect, in high school. There is too little focus on developing positive self-concepts and motivations to allow the student to overcome his history of failure.

Continuing and Adult Education

One of the difficulties encountered by community-junior colleges in applying the concept of "terminal education," as discussed in Chapter 1, was that no program actually terminated a person's learning. The emerging concept of continuing education reflects the pleasant fact that education is really a lifelong activity, in or out of school. Without special recruitment in most cases, the classrooms of community-junior colleges have been filling during the evening hours with adults anxious to upgrade their skills or to improve their personal lives. Most community-junior colleges claim a parttime evening student population as large as their fulltime day enrollment. Continuing and adult educational programs, furthermore, are not limited to evening courses. Special daytime courses and programs, on and off campus, serve special interests of the larger community (Medsker, 1960).

The adults come for many reasons. Some want regular college programs leading to eventual transfer to a four-year college or university or to employment; others seek recreational and cultural outlets. It is not uncommon to find a class on flower-arranging next to one on income-tax preparation, both across the hall from a class on symbolic logic.

Adult and continuing educational programs in community-junior colleges have expanded more from the pressure of numbers than from the special efforts of the colleges. With a constituency as large as the day enrollment, the offices of adult and continuing education often occupy some inconspicuous corner of the administration building, if indeed they are not exiled to some more remote spot. The proportion of the college budget allocated to adult and continuing education is correspondingly meager. Many students enter adult and continuing education programs excited at the prospect of going to, or returning to, college, only to find little college atmosphere prevailing outside the classroom in the evening. Quite possibly, the library, the bookstore, and the student center are not available to students at night.

At the same time, no area of the community-junior college curriculum is doing so well with so little. Despite meager resources, enrollment in adult and continuing education programs continues to soar. Faculty members generally enjoy teaching the older students, finding their maturity a good base for relevant and stimulating class discussions. Administrators know that valuable public relations, no small asset when tax or bond referendums are at stake, are generated by the adults attending adult programs. Most important of all, members of the community know that an opportunity exists for them to claim an education that has perhaps been long neglected, or to pursue various special interests in a college setting.

The Resulting Picture

From this overview of the salient characteristics and the general curricular programs in the nation's community-junior colleges, a composite picture emerges. Those who idealize this relative newcomer to American higher education can boast of its accomplishments, and skeptics can emphasize its shortcomings. By most standards, community-junior colleges have done an excellent job of implementing their multiple purposes and lofty goals. It is only when measured against their own claims that the performance of community-junior colleges appears substandard, a point noted in Medsker's national study in 1960. It is to the credit of community-junior colleges, however, that they continue to search for ways to improve their performance rather than ways to modify their goals or to lessen their commitments.

References

Blocker, Clyde E.; Plummer, Robert H.; and Richardson, Richard C., Jr. *The Two Year College: A Social Synthesis*. Englewood Cliffs, N.J.: Prentice-Hall, Inc., 1965.

Bogue, Jesse P. "The Community College." *American Association of University Professors' Bulletin*, XXXIV (June, 1948), 285–295.

Brubacher, John S. *Bases for Policy in Higher Education.* New York: McGraw-Hill Book Company, 1965.

Carnegie Commission on Higher Education. *Less Time, More Options: Education Beyond the High School.* New York: McGraw-Hill, 1971.

————. *The Open-Door Colleges: Policies for Community Colleges.* New York: McGraw-Hill Book Company, 1970.

Case, Chester H. "Beyond Evaluation: The Quality Control Model of Evaluation and the Development Model for Faculty Growth and Evaluation." Mimeographed, 1971.

Clark, Burton R. *The Open Door College.* New York: McGraw-Hill Book Company, 1960.

Cohen, Arthur M. *Dateline '79: Heretical Concepts for the Community College.* Beverly Hills: Glencoe Press, 1969.

Collins, C. C., and Collins, J. J. *The Case for the Community College: A Critical Appraisal of Philosophy and Function.* El Cajon, California: Published by the authors, 1966.

Conant, James B. *The American High School Today.* New York: McGraw-Hill Book Company, 1959.

Educational Policies Commission. *Universal Opportunity for Education Beyond the High School.* Washington, D.C.: National Educational Association, 1964.

Fordyce, Joseph W. "Faculty Development in American Community-Junior Colleges." *Peabody Journal of Education,* XLVIII (July, 1971), 270–275.

Garrison, R. H. *Junior College Faculty: Issues and Problems — A Preliminary National Appraisal.* Washington, D.C.: American Association of Junior Colleges, 1967.

Gleazer, Edmund J., Jr. "AAJC Approach — Project Focus: Some Impressions." *Junior College Journal,* XLII (August-September, 1971), 7–9. (A)

————. "The Emerging Role of the Community-Junior College." *Peabody Journal of Education,* XLVIII (July, 1971), 255–256.

————. *Student Personnel Work: A Senior Partner in the Junior College.* Paper presented at the First Annual Junior College Student Personnel Workshop, Dallas, Texas, April, 1967.

Harris, Norman. "The Middle Manpower Job Spectrum." In *Perspectives on the Community-Junior College.* (ed.) Ogilvie, W. K. and Raines, Max R. New York: Appleton-Century-Crofts, 1971, pp. 249–258.

Hillway, Tyrus. *The American Two-Year College.* New York: Harper and Brothers, 1958.

Huther, John W. "The Open Door: How Open Is It?" *Junior College Journal,* XLI (April, 1971), pp. 24–27.

Johnson, B. Lamar. *Islands of Innovation.* Junior College Leadership Program Occasional Report No. 6. Los Angeles: University of California, 1964.

————. *Islands of Innovation Expanding: Changes for the Community College.* Beverly Hills: Glencoe Press, 1969.

Kimball, John R. "Analysis of Institutional Objectives in Michigan's Community Colleges." Unpublished doctoral dissertation, Michigan State University, 1960.

Knoell, Dorothy M., and Medsker, Leland L. *From Junior to Senior College: A Study of the Transfer Student.* Washington, D.C.: American Council on Education, 1965.

Martin, Marie. "The Federal Government Behind the Open Door." *Peabody Journal of Education,* XLVIII (July, 1971), 282–285.

Matson, Jane E. "Student Personnel Services in Two-Year Colleges: A Time for Charting New Directions." *Peabody Journal of Education,* XLVIII (July, 1971), 276–281.

Maul, Ray C. "The Biggest Problem: Finding Good Teachers." *Junior College Journal,* XXXVI (December-January, 1965), 7–9.

Medsker, Leland L. *The Junior College: Progress and Prospect.* McGraw-Hill Book Company, 1960.

———— and Tillery, Dale. *Breaking the Access Barriers: A Profile of Two-Year Colleges.* New York: McGraw-Hill Book Company, 1971.

National Advisory Council on Education Professions Development. *First Annual Report to the President and the Congress of the United States.* Washington, D.C.: Mimeographed, 1968.

National Committee for Appraisal and Development of Junior College Student Personnel Programs. *A Report to the Carnegie Corporation of New York.* 1965.

O'Banion, Terry. "New Directions in Community Colleges." Champaign: mimeographed, 1969.

————. *New Directions in Community College Student Personnel Programs.* Student Personnel Series No. 15. Washington, D.C.: American College Personnel Association, 1971.

President's Commission on Higher Education. *Higher Education for American Democracy.* 6 Vols. Washington, D.C.: U.S. Government Printing Office, 1947.

President's Commission on National Goals. *Goals for Americans.* New York: Prentice-Hall, Inc., 1960.

President's Committee on Education Beyond the High School. *Second Report to the President.* Washington, D.C.: U.S. Government Printing Office, 1957.

President's Task Force on Higher Education. *Priorities in Higher Education.* Washington, D.C.: U.S. Government Printing Office, 1970.

Reynolds, James W. *The Comprehensive Junior College Curriculum.* Berkeley: McCutchan Publishing Corporation, 1969.

Rouche, John E. *Salvage, Redirection or Custody? Remedial Education in the Community-Junior College.* Washington, D.C.: American Association of Junior Colleges, 1968.

Schultz, Raymond E. "Curriculum Trends and Directions in American Junior Colleges." *Peabody Journal of Education,* XLVIII (July, 1971), 262–269.

Thornton, James W., Jr. *The Community-Junior College.* New York: John Wiley & Sons, 1966.

Tillery, Dale. "A College for Everyman." Mimeographed, 1970.

Wetzler, Wilson, F. "A Break-Through for Faculty and Program Development." *Junior College Journal,* XL (June-July, 1970), 13–15.

3. Community-Junior College Students

Attempts to describe typical community-junior college students face many of the same complexities confronting attempts to describe a typical community-junior college. Indeed, as the open-door image of the community-junior college attracts more and more students, diversity increases both within the college program and within the student body. Virtually all studies of community-junior college students point first to the *heterogeneity* of the student body, before advancing cautious generalizations about community-junior college students. Among the researched factors relating to the nature of this student population are *socioeconomic backgrounds, skill levels, personality characteristics ,*and individual *goals.* In this chapter, all of these factors will be briefly discussed, along with a discussion of the *social mixture* resulting from the makeup of community-junior college students, particularly in regard to minority students.

Heterogeneity

Most research on community-junior college students shows them to be representative of the total population in their communities (Medsker and Tillery, 1971). A reporter for *American Education* viewed the heterogeneity of community-junior college students thus:

If there is anything that characterizes junior and community colleges as phenomena of the sixties, it is the people attracted to the opportunities they offer. Junior college and community college students come from every walk of life. They are young, middle-aged, and old. They comprise all races and national origins. Most of them probably would never have seen the inside of a college classroom had not a two-year college been spawned in their immediate locale. The two-year colleges have brought together a somewhat incongruous assortment of classmates. It is not unusual to see a mini-skirted teenager studying alongside a middle-aged working man. Or a mother and son pursuing a two-year associate degree in the same program. Or a uniformed policeman trying to get law and order into his lecture notes. Typically, they are there to get something, although they don't always know what exactly it is they want. There's no good answer to the question: Who is the junior college student? The student is a housewife whose educational career was interrupted by marriage and family. Or a bright but poor youngster who works and studies while living at home. The student is a ghetto kid with limited opportunities, or a youngster whose middle-class family wants him closer to home for a couple of years before sending him away to the big university. The student may even be a doctor of philosophy, satisfying his curiosity about computers in an evening course or brushing up on art in a Saturday class. Perhaps the only answer is that the student is one of nearly two million people who are lapping up everything these colleges can put out. [*American Education,* 1968, p. 15.]

It is perhaps easier to appreciate the heterogeneity of the community-junior college student body through the eyes of a perceptive reporter than through statistics. Quantitative measures of student characteristics are difficult to gather and are often unreliable. The age distribution of community-junior college students, for example, has been determined in a recent study by Koos to be significantly different than the one reported in a national study by Medsker; Medsker reported that 53 percent of regular day-time students were twenty-two years of age or younger, while Koos determined from his data that 86 percent of regular day-time students fell in that age category (Medsker, 1960, p. 43; Koos, 1970, p. 7). Both Medsker and Koos agreed, however, that a majority of *all* community-junior college students, including part-time and night students, are twenty-one years of age or older. Since most of the research that has been done on community-junior college students has focused on the young adult between eighteen and twenty-two years of age, a significant segment of the community-junior college student population has been largely overlooked.

Male students in community-junior colleges outnumber female students at about the ratio of three to two. (Thornton, 1966.) In most vocational-technical programs, however, the ratio is much higher. The percentage of married students generally runs at the same level as it does for all college students nationwide — about 25 per cent (Wise, 1958; Medsker, 1960). Most studies report that 50 to 70 percent of community-junior college students work at outside jobs for ten hours or more per week.

It is perhaps more revealing to view the heterogeneity of community-junior college students in terms of student "types," of which there is no precise counting. The following list of eight student types by Medsker illustrates the usual blending of academic and motivational factors characteristic of students:

(1) The high school graduate of moderate ability and achievement who enters junior college right after high school as a fulltime student with the intention of transferring to a given institution with a particular major

(2) The low achiever in high school who "discovers" college quite late and then becomes highly motivated to enroll in a junior college transfer program for which he is not equipped, yet who may be a "late bloomer"

(3) The high school graduate of low ability who enters junior college because of social pressure or because he cannot find employment

(4) The very bright high school graduate who could have been admitted to a major university who may have low scores on measures of "intellectual disposition" and "social maturity"

(5) The intellectually capable but unmotivated, disinterested high school graduate who comes to junior college to "explore," hoping it will offer him what he does not know he is looking for

(6) The transfer (in) from a four-year college who either failed or withdrew after an unsatisfactory experience in a semester, a year, or more

(7) The high school dropout who probably comes from a minority group and a culturally disadvantaged family, with only grade-school level skills and a strong interest in securing vocational training

(8) The late college entrant (over 25) who was employed, in military service, or in the home for a number of years after high school and who now is motivated to pursue an associate (and perhaps a baccalaureate) degree, however long it may take. [Medsker, 1965-B, pp. 21–22.]

Medsker's typology, like most other typologies of community-junior college students (Blocker, Plummer, and Richardson, 1965; Hillway, 1958; Thornton, 1966), accentuates the background, skills, personality, and general characteristics of community-junior college students, areas in which lie crucial factors affecting the successes and failures of these students.

Socioeconomic Background

Researchers have discovered no variables related to college attendance with higher correlation than socioeconomic background variables such as father's occupation, income, and education. Table 3.1 shows how these variables correlate with type of college attended. For all three variables, private universities are at the top of the range and public two-year (community-junior) colleges are at or near the bottom. Although there are some discrepancies between the data drawn by Cross from two sources — the American Council on Education and Medsker and Trent's study — both collections of data reveal the lower educational and socioeconomic status of the families of community-junior college students. Other studies have confirmed that approximately 30 percent of the fathers of community-junior college students have had some college. Nearly 20 percent of the fathers, however, have no more than a grade-school education (Florida State Department of Education, 1962; Knoell and Medsker, 1964; Medsker and Trent, 1965-A).

Underneath these statistics lies the fundamental importance of family support, both financial and attitudinal, for college attendance. Regardless of the type of college attended, most college students have received strong encouragement from their families. Cross states that 66 prcent of four-year college students and 55 percent of community-junior college students report that their parents "wanted them to go to college for sure." This compares with only 26 percent of college non-goers who reported receiving similar attitudinal support for college attendance from their families. (Cross, 1968.) Trent and Medsker's study, which traced the paths of 10,000 high school graduates over a five-year period, showed that college persistence, as well as the decision to attend college, was related more to the socioeconomic background of the student than to his academic aptitude. These researchers concluded "that lack of family support with respect to higher education is related to a forfeiting of educational opportunities, and that schools compensate little for missing parental interest" (Trent and Medsker, 1969).

TABLE 3.1

**Relation Between Socioeconomic Background
and Type of College Attended (in Percentages)**

Type of College	Fathers With College*	Fathers With College**	Family Income Over $10,000**	Fathers — Professional or Managerial*
Private University	64	61	64	49
Private Four-year	63		60	
Catholic Four-year	54	32	54	43
Protestant Four-year	51		51	
Public University	49	49	49	35
Private Two-year	39	39	42	20
Public Four-year	34	31	33	19
Public Two-year	34	29	40	16

*Based on ACE data
**Based on Medsker-Trent data

[Cross, 1968, p. 15.]

Community-junior colleges serve all types of students, but they seem to play a special role for students with lower socioeconomic backgrounds. A nationwide study of community-junior college honor students by Schultz revealed that two-thirds of the successful student group came from families of "blue collar" fathers. The fathers of two-thirds of the honor students had had no college whatsoever, and nearly 25 percent of them had not progressed beyond the eighth grade (Schultz, 1967). According to Schultz's study, then, success in a community-junior college is not significantly related to higher socioeconomic levels of student backgrounds. Once in a community-junior college, students with lower socioeconomic backgrounds who are "new" to higher education have a real opportunity to success.

For this new student in higher education, the existence of a community-junior college is essential. Medsker and Trent have noted that the presence or absence of a community-junior college in a community weighs heavily in the determination of whether or not many high school graduates can go on to a successful college experience:

A factor which clearly had a bearing on whether certain graduates went immediately to college was the type of public college, if any, in the community. As had been hypothesized, graduates in communities with public junior colleges were the most likely to continue their education and the communities with state colleges were next in order. The relative impact of the junior college on young people from low socioeconomic homes, particularly with high ability, was striking. [Medsker and Trent, 1965-A, p. 100.]

Skill Levels

There is no shortage of information about how community-junior college students score on tests of academic aptitude and ability, but there is a great need for caution in interpreting the scores. All researchers confirm that community-junior college students, compared to their counterparts in four-year colleges and universities, score significantly lower on all current measures of academic ability. When considering the meaning of these measures, however, two important qualifications must be made. One has been stated by Cross as follows:

Present tests are, on the whole, effective measures of success in the traditional curriculum, and it comes as no surprise that the student oriented toward traditional education scores higher on the test oriented in the same direction. . . . Very little is known about the matter of special abilities and aptitudes of the junior college student, new to the ranks of higher education. We need to explore the strengths of this student and to expand our dimensions of measurement. [Cross, 1968, pp. 47–48.]

A second important consideration is that statistical "averages" conceal the extraordinarily wide range of abilities of community-junior college students. It may be more appropriate for selective, four-year colleges and universities to compare such averages since their student populations tend to be more academically homogeneous than those of community-junior colleges. If one keeps these two cautionary notes in mind, the abundant statistical data on the academic skills of community-junior college students shrink in significance.

Compared to the general population, the academic skills of community-junior college students appear quite normal. It is only when compared to four-year college and university students, as in Table 3.2, that community-junior college students appear academically disadvantaged.

TABLE 3.2

Academic Ability of Community-Junior College Students Compared to Students at Four-Year Colleges and Universities (by Quartiles)

Type of Student	First Quartile (Highest)	Second Quartile	Third Quartile	Fourth Quartile (Lowest)
Four-Year & University	59%	26%	11%	4%
Community-Junior College	20%	31%	32%	17%

(Adapted from data in Medsker and Tillery, 1971, p. 42.)

Other studies reveal similar distributions of academic ability within the community-junior college student body — distributions that are closer to representing high school seniors than other four-year college and university students (Seashore, 1958; Seibel, 1965; Koos, 1970).

The distribution of community-junior college students in regard to academic ability is as widespread as in regard to socioeconomic background. The following charts divide both family occupational level and academic ability into four categories, revealing a substantial percentage of community-junior college students in each category:

FIGURE 3.1

Characteristics of Students in Two-Year Colleges

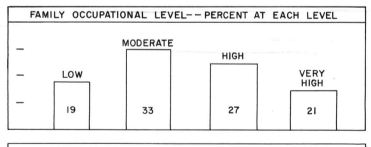

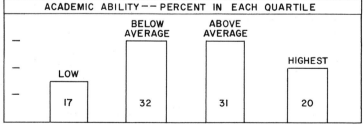

SOURCE: Surveys conducted in four states (California, Illinois, Massachusetts, and North Carolina) by SCOPE PROJECT, Center for Research and Development in Higher Education, University of California, Berkeley.   [Carnegie Commission on Higher Education, 1970, p. 4.]

FIGURE 3.2

Overlap in ACE Scores of Freshmen Entering Two-Year and Four-Year Colleges (in Percentages)

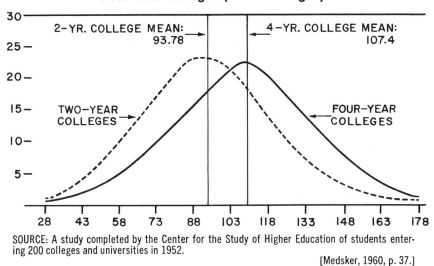

SOURCE: A study completed by the Center for the Study of Higher Education of students entering 200 colleges and universities in 1952.

[Medsker, 1960, p. 37.]

One must continually guard against the conclusion that community-junior college students have lesser abilities than do four-year college and university students; the point is that they have *different* abilities. As stated previously, almost all data on community-junior college student skills are reported in terms of traditional measures that are inappropriate measures of success in many community-junior college programs. If one were to compare simply the type of community-junior college student who registers in the highest academic quartile with four-year college and university students, there would be few if any academic differences. In California, for instance, where a high school graduate must be in the upper 12.5 percent of his class to qualify for admission to a state university, 18 percent of the students eligible choose instead to attend a community-junior college. Reference to the fact that only 26 percent of eligible students actually do attend the state universities makes it obvious that in California large numbers of academically successful students attend community-junior colleges (Tillery, 1964). The considerable overlap of academic abilities among students of two-year and four-year colleges can be seen in Figure 3.2.

It must be regretted, however, that research on the skills of community-junior college students has neglected to inventory special skills — mechanical, coping, social, artistic, etc. — which may be useful in distinguishing types of students and planning programs for them. Data on academic ability are universally collected by schools and colleges, and are, of course, the most readily available information for research. There exists a pressing need, however, to go beyond these data and to find new measures of value for assessing the community-junior college student population.

Personality Characteristics

"In general, junior college students are more conventional, less independent, less attracted to reflective thought, and less tolerant than their peers in four-year institutions" (Cross, 1968, p. 32). This statement sums up much of what is known about the personality characteristics of community-junior college students, and again it is a comparative measure with four-year students. It is based mostly upon data for regular daytime students, and thus neglects the considerable student population in community-junior colleges over twenty-two years of age. And, once again, it is based on the "average student," although in fact community-junior college students are composed of various groupings which lose important identifying traits when merged.

A survey of 250,000 college freshmen by the American Council on Education in the fall of 1966 asked the students to rate themselves as above or below average in a variety of traits. As a group, community-junior college students were less confident than four-year college and university freshmen in reference to such traits as academic ability, leadership ability, mathematical ability, intellectual self-confidence, and writing ability. Slightly larger proportions of community-junior college students than four-year college students felt themselves above average in athletic ability, artistic ability, defensiveness, and mechanical ability (Table 3.3).

Medsker and Tillery also reported on their SCOPE data (School to College Opportunities for Post-secondary Education), revealing that the self-concepts of most community-junior college students exhibit less self-confidence than those of other college students:

SCOPE findings, to date, suggest that many junior college youths are marginal students, not only because of economic pressures and lack of incentives at home, but because they themselves are not sure they can make it. Compared to their peers at senior colleges, they have had only modest success in high school, less than satisfying guidance experiences, and continuing doubts about their ability to do college work. . . . whereas 71 percent of the 1966 SCOPE seniors who went to independent universities *definitely* believed they could do college work, 71 percent of the public junior college students had doubts about their capabilities [Medsker and Tillery, p. 83].

Community-junior college students tend to be motivated less by intellectual than by practical considerations. When stating their reasons for

TABLE 3.3

Students Rating Themselves "Above Average" On ACE Survey Traits (in Percentages)

	Two-Year Colleges	Four-Year Colleges	Universities
Academic ability	37	61	69
Athletic ability	37	35	37
Artistic ability	19	18	20
Cheerfulness	54	54	54
Defensiveness	29	27	28
Drive to achieve	47	59	63
Leadership ability	29	39	44
Mathematical ability	24	36	44
Mechanical ability	27	22	27
Originality	32	37	42
Political conservatism	12	16	17
Political liberalism	13	20	22
Popularity (general)	27	32	36
Popularity (opposite sex)	27	28	32
Public speaking ability	16	23	26
Self-confidence (intellectual)	27	36	43
Self-confidence (social)	29	29	32
Sensitivity to criticism	23	28	29
Stubbornness	36	36	39
Understanding of others	56	61	62
Writing ability	19	29	32

[Cross, 1968, p. 26.]

college attendance, the majority of community-junior college students give first place to considerations such as location, low cost and nearness to home, whereas a larger percentage of four-year and university students listed an intellectual atmosphere, good faculty, and high scholastic standing as predominant reasons for their college choice (Knoell and Medsker, 1954; Cross, 1968).

Not only do many community-junior college students enter college with attitudes generally considered less than appropriate for intellectual pursuits and full personality development, but their personality traits actually seem to counteract attempts of community-junior colleges to make them more openminded and more aware of their social and cultural environment. Telford and Plant compared junior college students attending college with applicants who decided not to attend college, and they found that the group attending college showed no significant differences in the development of autonomy and tolerance in comparison to the control group (Telford and Plant, 1963). Of course, there was a bias in this study since the control group had actually applied to a community-junior college and could be quite different from most college nongoers. Trent and Medsker found that all colleges, including community-junior colleges, do assist in the development of individual autonomy as measured by various psychological tests. Moreover, they found significant differences in the level of autonomy reached by college persisters compared to dropouts, and by dropouts compared to non-attenders, again regardless of the type of college. In a conclusion that is especially significant for community-junior colleges, Trent and Medsker stated:

... it appears that below average ability, a limited educational background, an autocratic and unstimulating family life, restricted economic opportunities, and an authoritarian religious subculture may have served as forces constricting growth of social maturity for a great many negative changers [Trent and Medsker, 1969, p. 218].

Thus the charge of community-junior colleges to educate students from low socioeconomic backgrounds who are less than intellectually inclined is not an easy one. Still, the community-junior college philosophy accepts that all young adults can develop better self-concepts and a fuller awareness of their social and cultural surroundings. For the traditional college student, this type of development is less difficult than for the "new student" in higher education. There is no evidence, however, that this difficulty is insurmountable.

Goals

Compared with students at four-year colleges and universities, community-junior college students tend to state their goals in more practical vocational terms. But, while their goals are stated practically, they often tend to be unrealistic, reflecting little appreciation of occupational requirements and personal abilities. Table 3.4, taken from SCOPE data, shows how aspirations of non-college, four-year college, and community-junior college students vary according to their fathers' occupational status.

While one-third of community-junior college students come from families in which the head of the household is in a managerial or professional classification, two-thirds of the students aspire to the higher status. Unfortunately, the most naive views often govern the thinking of upward aspiring students. Olsen's study of several hundred community-junior college students concluded that few recognized the difference between "liking" an activity and actually "performing" it. Furthermore, Olsen uncovered an alarming lack of knowledge among the students about the occupations of their choice (Olsen, 1960).

Douvan and Kaye report that college students in general often harbor collegiate goals which are unrealistic. Girls often foresee romantic goals involving men and marriage while boys envision a position of social status and wealth (Douvan and Kaye, 1962). Community-junior college students are certainly not exempt from such dreaming. There are some who argue that a real exposure to the "world of work" would bring such youthful idealism into a more realistic perspective. Medsker and Trent, however, in their longitudinal study of 10,000 high school graduates, found that the most unrealistic attitudes toward occupational goals existed among the group who did not enter college and went right to work. And those who dropped out of college, according to the researchers, were less realistic about their own futures than those remaining in college (Trent and Medsker, 1969). So it may be true that college students are naive about their own potentials and goals, but it should not be assumed that a proper cure is to push them into the world of work.

TABLE 3.4

Student's Occupational Aspiration Compared With Father's Occupational Status (in Percentages)

Occupational Level	Non-College	Junior College	Four-Year College
Unskilled occupations			
Father's status	42	23	17
Student's aspiration	14	6	1
Skilled and semi-professional occupations			
Father's status	36	45	33
Student's aspiration	49	30	10
Managerial and professional occupations			
Father's status	23	32	50
Student's aspiration	36	64	89

[Cross, 1968, p. 46.]

Studies of community-junior college students universally report that these students are more "practically-oriented" than their counterparts at four-year colleges and universities. However, the SCOPE study asked students: "At the present time, do you think of your education more as an opportunity to become skilled in a particular line of work, or more as an opportunity to receive a general education?" Community-junior college students responded:

Entirely general education 7%
Mostly general education 43%
Mostly job training 36%
Entirely job training 9%
[Cross, 1968, p. 36.]

A majority of community-junior college students, then, clearly perceived their collegiate opportunity as much broader than simply vocational. However, occupational education aiming toward higher status occupations might very well include a natural emphasis upon general education in the early college years.

Altogether, very little is known about why community-junior college students aspire to the positions they do. Burton Clark suspects that general societal pressure for upward mobility is a root cause (Clark, 1960). The recurring tendency for these students to select transfer programs, at a ratio of two-to-one, over occupational-vocational programs reveals very clearly their social aspirations. The efforts of counseling and guidance notwithstanding, the socially prestigious bachelor's degree has been a primary goal for several generations of community-junior college students.

The Social Mix

American institutions of higher education in recent years have become painfully aware of the few minority students within their classrooms. As four-year colleges and universities have struggled to make their student populations reflect to a greater degree the general population mix of the larger society, community-junior colleges have been able to pride themselves on their better record. Such pride is justified, but statistics show that minority enrollments in community-junior colleges are not overwhelming (See Table 3.5). In urban areas, the portion of minority groups in community-junior colleges is much higher than the national average (See Table 3.6).

The community-junior colleges are doing a fair job, compared to other institutions of higher education, in enrolling students from minority groups. It is another question altogether to ask to what extent the community-junior colleges provide relevant programs for these students. Medsker and Tillery have reported these examples of colleges trying to meet the challenges:

Cleveland. Before the first permanent building was constructed, Cuyahoga College had "store-front" guidance centers in the black communities of the central city.

San Mateo. A largely white college went out to seek minority students and paid them to learn. Although the community college had difficulties living up to its promises, it recruited a talented and unconventional staff which "turned on" many ghetto students. . . .

New York City. With support from the Office of Economic Opportunity and supervision from the American Association of Junior Colleges, the Brooklyn Urban Center of CCNY is reaching out to serve the parents of Head Start children — to help them become involved in the education of their own children and to explore new careers for themselves.

Chicago. What is now Malcolm X College is taking English as a second language into the homes of black citizens and Spanish-speaking immigrants. In doing so, it is developing tutors and teachers from the minority communities served by the program. [Medsker and Tillery, 1971, pp. 80–81.]

But many community-junior colleges merely treat minority students as disadvantaged students, trying through remedial programs to force them into a pattern of learning that has never proved successful for them. According to Andrew L. Goodrich, minority students should be considered "oppressed" rather than "disadvantaged." Programs should be constructed to remove oppression and build upon potentials rather than to emphasize weaknesses (Goodrich, 1971). Clarke and Ammons have shown that at one Florida junior college the SCAT (School and College Ability Test), which proved a good predictor of college success for whites, and to a lesser extent for Negro females, had no predictive ability for Negro males. Measures of student self-concepts, the researchers went on to demonstrate, were better predictors for all students (Clark and Ammons, 1970). But many community-junior colleges, not to mention other institutions of higher education, on the basis of such tests continue to place minority students into remedial programs, too many of which are negatively conceived.

TABLE 3.5

Racial Composition of Enrollments in Public Junior Colleges (in Percentages)

Race	SCOPE* 1967	Creager† 1968	CGP*† 1969
Caucasian	84	84	84
Negro	8	9	8
Oriental	2	2	3
Other	6	5	(5)

*SOURCE: Respondents to 1967 SCOPE College Questionnaire. Eleven percent identified self as mixture of racial/ethnic groups or chose not to respond. Data adjusted by assigning ⅓ of this group to Negro, ⅓ to Caucasian, and ⅓ to "Other." Caucasian includes Mexican-American.

†SOURCE: Creager et al., 1968. Adjusted by rounding; adding ½ of "Other" to Negro because of black response to that term; and adding American Indian to "Other."

*†SOURCE: Cross, 1969. The 5 per cent in the "Other" category has been added to Cross's reporting of these comparative Guidance and Placement Program data.

[Medsker and Tillery, 1971, p. 76.]

Community-junior colleges must do more to establish viable programs for their minority students; they must do more to use the social mixture of their student population to promote social understandings; and, further, they must do more to increase the number of minority students on their campuses. Knoell has conducted extensive interviews with inner-city black youth who were not attending college. She discovered that two-thirds of them recognized the importance of an immediate college education. Only 10 percent expressed no interest in attending college (Knoell, 1969).

TABLE 3.6

Representation of Minority Groups in Urban Community-Junior Colleges (in Percentages)

College	Enrollment*	Caucasian	Negro	Other
City College of San Francisco	12,438	71.1	10.8	18.1
Los Angeles City College	10,476	51.0	26.6	22.4
City Colleges of Chicago	13,115	69.9	27.8	2.3
District of St. Louis	10,121	85.6	14.0	.4
El Centro College (Dallas)	6,053	81.8	14.0	4.2

*Based on 1967–68 enrollments.

[Carnegie Commission on Higher Education, 1970, Appendix A.]

Conclusion

All too little is known about the students in community-junior colleges and about those who should be there, but are not. Information is often based on measures inappropriate for the community-junior college student population. Specific data about adult students and minority students are on the whole lacking. At present, there are more dangers than advantages in conceptualizing the "average community-junior college student." It is probably better, until data are more nearly complete, to hold an impressionistic view of community-junior college students not unlike the one of the reporter quoted at the beginning of this chapter. There is not *a* community-junior college student, but rather there are many types — the traditional freshmen and sophomores, the older adults, the "new" students, the minority students, and so on. The community-junior college student population, like the movement itself, is too complex to stereotype.

References

Blocker, Clyde E.; Plummer, Robert H.; and Richardson, Richard C., Jr. *The Two-Year College: A Social Synthesis.* Englewood Cliffs, N.J.: Prentice-Hall, Inc., 1965.

Clark, Burton R. *The Open Door College.* New York: McGraw-Hill Book Company, 1960.

Clarke, Johnnie R. and Ammons, Rose Mary. "Identification and Diagnosis of Disadvantaged Students." *Junior College Journal,* XL (February, 1970), 13–17.

Cross, K. Patricia. *The Junior College Student: A Research Description.* Educational Testing Service, 1968.

Douvan, Elizabeth and Kaye, Carol. "Motivational Factors in College Entrance." In Nevitt Sanford, ed., *The American College.* New York: John Wiley & Sons, 1962, 199–224.

Florida State Department of Education. *Florida's Community Junior Colleges: Their Contributions and Their Future.* Report by the Task Force on the Junior College Student. Tallahassee: State Junior College Advisory Board, 1962.

Goodrich, Andrew L. "The Now Faculty and the New Student." *Junior College Journal,* XLI (May, 1971), 26–29.

Hillway, Tyrus. *The American Two-Year College.* New York: Harper & Brothers, Publishers, 1958.

Knoell, Dorothy M. "Who Goes to College in the Cities." *Junior College Journal,* XL (September, 1969), 23–27.

———— and Medsker, Leland L. *Factors Affecting Performance of Transfer Students From Two- to Four-Year Colleges.* Cooperative Research Project No. 2167. Berkeley: University of California, Center for the Study of Higher Education, 1964.

Koos, Leonard V. *The Community College Student.* Gainesville: University of Florida Press, 1970.

Medsker, Leland L. *The Junior College: Progress and Prospect.* McGraw-Hill Book Company, 1960.

————and Tillery, Dale. *Breaking the Access Barriers: A Profile of Two-Year Colleges.* New York: McGraw-Hill Book Company, 1971.

————. "The Junior College Student." In *Junior College Student Personnel Programs: Appraisal and Development.* A Report to the Carnegie Corporation, November, 1965. (B)

———— and Trent, James W. *The Influence of Different Types of Higher Institutions of College Attendance from Varying Socio-Economic and Ability Levels.* Cooperative Research Project No. 438. Berkeley: University of California, Center for Research and Development in Higher Education, 1965. (A)

Olsen, L. R. "Junior College Student's Reasons for Occupational Choice." *Junior College Journal,* XXX (March, 1960), 396–399.

Seashore, Harold. "Academic Abilities of Junior College Students." *Junior College Journal,* XXIX (October, 1958), 74–80.

Schultz, Raymond E. "A Follow-Up on Honor Students." *Junior College Journal,* XXXVIII (December, 1967), 9–15.

Siebel, Dean W. *A Study of the Academic Ability and Performance of Junior College Students.* Princeton, N.J.: Educational Testing Service, 1965.

Telford, Charles W. and Plant, Walter T. *The Psychological Impact of the Public Two-Year College on Certain Non-Intellectual Functions.* Cooperative Research Project No. 914. Washington, D.C.: U.S. Office of Education, 1963.

Thornton, James W., Jr. *The Community Junior College.* New York: John Wiley & Sons, 1966.

Tillery, Dale H. "Differential Characteristics of Entering Freshmen at the University of California and Their Peers at California Junior Colleges." Unpublished doctoral dissertation, University of California, 1964.

Trent, James W. and Medsker, Leland L. *Beyond High School.* San Francisco: Jossey-Bass, 1969.

Wise, Max W. *They Come for the Best of Reasons — College Students Today.* Washington, D.C.: American Council on Education, 1958.

4. The People Who Staff the People's College

The community-junior college has often been called the "people's college." This term indicates the unique role in equalizing post high school education opportunities for all Americans who desire such education.

The Carnegie Commission has supported the expansion of the "people's college." By 1980, the Commission hopes that community-junior colleges will be within commuting distance of about 95 percent of all Americans. The Commission also hopes that community-junior colleges will retain their "people's" role through the provision of comprehensive educational services for all students.

If history follows the Carnegie Commission's recommendations, then 1980's community-junior college will strongly resemble its 1971 progenitor. It will be filled with heterogeneous students to whom it will offer a wide range of programs. In 1980, as in the 1970s, the community-junior college will attempt to serve many different parts of its community with these programs.

The success or failure of the community-junior college in 1980 rests on the same base as it did in the 1970s — the quality of the teaching staff. As early as 1931, Eells proclaimed that the community-junior college "has little or no excuse for existence if it does not place prime emphasis on superior teaching, superior instructors, and superior methods of instruction." In 1960, Thornton agreed that "either (the community-junior college) teaches excellently or it fails completely." This emphasis upon quality teaching has echoed so loudly in the community-junior college rhetoric that this institution has become known as the "teaching college."

This section of the report examines the "people's college" from the standpoint of the "teaching college." It examines the nature of 1971's community-junior college staff, especially teaching staff, in order to make recommendations for the community-junior college of 1980. The staff is the primary focus here because, to paraphrase Evans' remarks in 1970:

... if we ask ourselves about the relative importance of the things that money can buy or create in community-junior college education, we quickly get down to buildings, curriculum, students and staff. ... Good colleges have been operated in poor buildings or no buildings at all. A good staff will create a good curriculum and will attract and retain good community-junior college students. But without a capable staff you simply do not have a college.

Characteristics of Staff

The following comments describe some of the extrinsic characteristics of community-junior college staff members. The descriptions attempt to characterize a "typical" staff member. However, like all statistical descriptions they fail to identify any one real entity. As Jung says:

The statistical method shows the facts in the light of the ideal average but does not give us a picture of their empirical reality. While reflecting an indisputable aspect of reality it can falsify the actual truth in a most misleading way.... The distinctive thing about real facts ... is their individuality. [1958, 17.]

This individuality-reality has been noted in the case of the community-junior college student (Medsker, 1964). It should be noted again in the case of the staff member. As Brower says, the community-junior college is "an institution where a heterogeneous student body meets a [equally] heterogeneous faculty (Kelly and Connolly, 1970).

Most community-junior college faculty are between 31 and 50 years of age. Medsker and Tillery state that less than 18 percent are under 30 and only 23 per cent are over 50. Siehr's 1961 study indicates that 35 percent are under 30 and only 7 percent are over 50. Thus community-junior colleges may have employed slightly older faculty in 1971 than in 1961.

Schultz, writing in 1965, shows that major administrative officers — presidents, academic deans, chief student personnel officers, and business officers — are usually older than most faculty. This characteristic is especially true for presidents and academic deans. Major administrative officers in private colleges are older than their public college counterparts.

Although no data are readily available, Medsker and Tillery believe that few community-junior college staff members are from minority ethnic groups. Also, " the social class background of many white staff members makes it difficult for them to relate to students from various ethnic groups." The National Science Foundation in 1967 has stated that only 30 percent of the community-junior college professional staff members are women. This percentage is also cited by Beazley in his 1966 and 1967 Higher Education General Information Survey reports.

Most community-junior college staff members have earned master's degrees. Among instructional staff, the general proportion seems to be 7:75:18 for bachelor's: master's: doctor's. This proportion is derived from the results of several studies (See Appendix A). The studies show that the proportion of instructors with the bachelor's, master's and doctor's degrees has remained fairly constant over the past ten years. Data for non-teaching staff indicate that most administrators and service staff hold master's degrees but the doctorate is more evident among presidents and academic deans (Anderson and Spencer, 1967, 1968; Schultz, 1965).

Despite their generally high level of education, few staff members have been oriented to the community-junior college through attendance as students in such institutions or through enrollment in a graduate course about such institutions (Medsker and Tillery, 1971). In Medsker and Tillery's study, only 8 percent of the staff had attended community-junior colleges as students and only 33 percent had taken courses about two-year colleges.

Community-junior college staff members are recruited from a wide range of sources, including primary and secondary schools, two-year colleges, four-year institutions, graduate schools, business and industry. The results of several studies about sources (Appendix B) indicate that public school systems provide the largest new community-junior college faculty. Business, industry, and other sources rank second, and community-junior colleges rank third as a source for new faculty. Schultz's data in 1965 indicate that most major administrators come from community-junior colleges; chief academic and student personnel officers are often promoted from the staffs of the same community-junior college.

The community-junior college staff member encounters a different job marketplace than his four-year college counterpart (Kelly and Connolly, 1970). The market is usually regional or statewide rather than national. Phair reports that 90 percent of California's new faculty have been recruited from within the state during the last four years (1970). Most job vacancies are new positions; the turnover of staff is about 16 percent per year. Conversely, most staff are new to their jobs; over 46 percent have been in the same job for three or less years (Medsker and Tillery, 1971).

The new community-junior college staff member may or may not have to be certified by the state in which he is employed. In 1966, nine states required specific teacher certification of at least a master's degree or equivalent experience in the subjct to be taught. Twenty-four states indicated no special community-junior college certification requirements (A.A.J.C., *To Work*, 1966).

So far, this report has mentioned several characteristics of 1971 faculty which resemble those of the 1960s. Medsker's study, *The Junior College: Progress and Prospect,* indicates that most of 1960s two-year college faculty were white collar or farm-family males who had taught previously in public schools. These faculty had master's degrees and they may or may not have been certified by the state in which they were employed. Thus, perhaps, several faculty characteristics are beginning to stabilize as historically typical characteristics of two-year college staffs.

The 1971 staff member's salary was usually affected by his college's size, geographic location, and control — public or private. Graybeal (1968) indicates that the larger the college, the larger the faculty member's salary. Regionally, faculty in Southeast colleges earn the least; faculty in Far West colleges earn the most. In 1968, public college faculty earned a median $9,165 per year while private college faculty earned just $7,211 per year (Simon and Grant, 1968).

The faculty member's salary is primarily based on education hours and work experience. Graybeal indicates that the median salary level for education and work is the "master's but less than six years." Salaries vary as much as −10 percent for less than a master's to +36 percent for a doctorate.

The community-junior college faculty member earns less than his four-year college counterpart (Medsker and Tillery, 1971). He also earns less than his own administrative colleagues. In Graybeal's statistics, no administrative median salary was lower than the faculty median. (1968)

In summary then, the "typical" community-junior college faculty member is a 31 to 50 year-old middle-class white male whose previous work experience has been in the public schools or in business and industry. He has a master's degree in his subject area. His course work has been taken at four-year institutions exclusively; it has seldom included the study of the community-junior college. This lack of experience in the academic field and in work is compounded by the faculty member's relatively recent entry into a community-junior college position, a new position that he may have found by chance in his local region.

This "typical" faculty member works with major administrators at his college. In general, those administrators are older, better paid, more educated and more experienced in community-junior college work than he.

Attitudes Toward the Community-Junior College

The characteristics of the typical faculty member indicate that he is vocationally and educationally unprepared for specific employment in the community-junior college. The following studies attempt to probe deeper into the staff member's attitudes toward his college and its students. Medsker and Tillery indicate that a study of attitudes is important because "if the staff [attitudes are] not in harmony with the expectations held for the community college, those expectations may not be realized" (1971).

Prior vocational-educational experiences seem to play a major role in the determination of the staff member's attitudes toward the college. Kelly and Connolly have stated:

Faculty from various sources can be typed according to their attitude and their demonstrated commitment to the two-year college. Future research may more clearly reveal differences that cannot be ignored, but a generalization can be made now: attitudes toward and commitment to the junior college as a place to work are tempered by previous occupational experience. [1970, 11.]

Friedman in 1967 classified two-year college instructors according to their previous occupational-educational experiences. Friedman's classifications include high schoolers, graduate students and professors. High schoolers come from the public school systems. They are subject-matter oriented and proudly disdainful of teaching methods. Graduate students have just left school. They are not especially committed to teaching as a career. They see the community-junior college as a stepping stone to bigger and better jobs or, failing that, more graduate study. Professors have previously taught undergraduates at four-year institutions. To them, the community-junior college symbolizes their permanent demotion in professional status.

Faculty with different backgrounds of experience have different reactions to the community-junior college. In Friedman's study, none of those reactions could be considered helpful to the college. Other studies seem to reinforce a general conclusion that many faculty members are not in favor of the comprehensive "people's college." These studies also seem to show that a faculty member's acceptance or non-acceptance of the community-junior college is related to the "academic" nature of his teaching role.

In 1967, Hamill reported that academic subject instructors with high academic preparation were dissatisfied with their community-junior colleges; they regarded four-year colleges and universities as their primary reference groups. Hunt discovered that "high potential" instructors of academic subjects were more four-year college oriented than "low potential" vocational education instructors who favored expansion of the comprehensive nature of community-junior colleges. (Cohen, 1971.)

Medsker and Tillery discovered that 44.4 percent of the two-year college staff members in their study would prefer to work in a four-year institution. Teachers of academic subjects were more traditional and less open to comprehensive college programs than vocational-education teachers, counselors, and administrators.

Often the bias toward academic traditionalism is directed toward low or marginal-ability students at two-year colleges. Daniels' survey of psychology instructors, Garrison's survey of general faculty, and Cohen's informal observations of UCLA teacher trainees have revealed a broad faculty distaste for working with low or marginal-ability students (Cohen and Brawer, 1971). Unfortunately, this distaste may build a defeatist attitude in students and a defensive attitude in faculty. The faculty may find it "easier . . . to accept the possibility that students may have personal barriers to learning than to recognize that we as teachers often defend against real change in ourselves" (Cohen and Brawer, 1971).

Unfortunately, some of these attitudes may also be historically "typical" of two-year college faculty. Medsker indicated that many of 1960's faculty preferred to work in four-year colleges or universities. (Medsker, 1960). Academic subject instructors were less inclined than administrators or vocational subject instructors [1960] to approve of "comprehensive" community-junior college programs.

The Impact of Graduate Preparation

Two-year college academic faculty are more prone to traditionalism than vocational faculty. A basic reason for this difference may be the academic preparation of these faculty. Garrison (*Issues,* 1967) reports:

As a wide generalization, those teachers most satisfied with their preparation for junior college instruction were those in the vocational areas since, as many of these pointed out, considerable work experience was required of them as a condition of employment by the college. On the other hand, liberal arts instructors (including many in the sciences) were inclined to be critical of their graduate work as "inadequate" or "inappropriate" or "not especially relevant" to the teaching situations in two-year colleges. The most general criticism was that graduate courses are too often slanted toward the needs of the prospective Ph.D., both in content and in treatment.

Community-junior college administrators have also voiced criticism of academic graduate training. Fordyce in 1970 summarized the administrators' views that:

community-junior colleges have been required to a very large extent to remold and remake university graduates in order that they could perform adequately as teachers at the community-college level. The emphasis upon research and other non-teaching functions and the insistence upon an ever increasing degree of specialization in the graduate schools of our nation has largely had a neutral if not actual, negative influence upon the preparation of graduate students for the function of teaching and counseling in America's community colleges.

An American Association of Junior Colleges' survey revealed the opinions of 288 community-junior college senior administrators about the needs for faculty inservice education and, thus, the weaknesses in faculty preservice graduate preparation. The faculty's greatest general need was for more preparation in "education, curriculum and learning" — including programmed instruction, testing and measurement, and learning theory. The greatest specific need was for a course concerning "The Philosophy, History, and Goals of the Two-Year College." Other high-ranking needs were for improved faculty preparation in remedial and ethnic studies, popular vocational education programs, and group dynamics and human relations.

These administrators seemed to agree completely that present college inservice training programs are not filling the gaps in instructor preservice preparation. Ninety-five percent of the respondents declared that the inservice "training which their people needed was *not* adequately available within their regions at least at the present time." The A.A.J.C. concluded that a "serious national 'training gap'" existed in the preparation and inservice development of two-year college faculty. (*In-Service,* 1969.)

The lack of adequate preparation does not ease as the faculty member gains more graduate credits. In fact, the problems of specialization and non-teaching orientation increase:

The fact is that the traditional Ph.D. program neglects appropriate training for undergraduate teaching even in a university. . . . The benefits of specialization are real and worthy of support, but they are only indirectly useful in many kinds of undergraduate instruction. The more nearly a Ph.D. realizes the potential of his specialized training, the less frequently he encounters undergraduates — even if he desires such encounters. This is a universal truth, and I see no point in pretending that it needs elaboration. [Rice, 1971, letter.]

As Garrison says, "the making of a scholar is the non-making of a teacher."

As a faculty member accumulates graduate credits, he may strengthen his prejudices against the community-junior college and its students. Chronister (1970) has stated that universities do not understand the purposes and problems of the two-year college in American society. Many university faculty believe that the community-junior college is a stop-gap pseudo-higher education institution (Garrison, *Issues,* 1967). These opinions may be reflected in graduate courses. Also, they may be reflected in the behavior of graduate faculty who act as teacher models for potential community-junior college faculty.

Apparently, the anti-community-junior college implications of graduate education are being recognized in two-year colleges. Collins and Tillery see no indication of an increase in faculty Ph.D.'s despite the present market surplus of potential teachers (1971). In his 1967 study, *Issues,* Garrison reports a faculty recognition of the inadequacies of the Ph.D. and, consequently, a movement away from the traditional degree.

Unfortunately, many universities have not recognized the limitations of their present attitudes and programs relating to the community-junior college. Even among the 200+ colleges and universities which are aware of the two-year college teacher's special graduate needs, many "innovative" programs have been nothing more than "verbal or administrative shufflings of the same graduate process, for individual requirements were changed little, if at all, to meet the new and expanded demands of training teachers," according to Garrison. As Blake said in 1971, "present programs for community college instructors are nothing more than the old graduate smorgasbord with the addition of a new dish generally entitled, 'the community college'."

This section has concentrated, so far, upon the deficiencies in graduate education for two-year college teachers of academic subjects. In so doing, it has reiterated the more general views of The President's Task Force on Higher Education. The Task Force noted in 1970 several problem areas in the improvement of the quality of the curriculum and methods of teaching and learning in higher education. Among those areas are:

(1) High professionalization of subject matter and high specialization of faculty members — both stemming from obvious sources and serving obvious needs, but also complicating needed adjustments in teaching and learning processes.

(2) Just as patterns of undergraduate education need reexamination, patterns in graduate education need to be revised. In many fields, over-professionalization has resulted in excessive, unproductive reliance on traditional forms of graduate work. A reevaluation of the purposes for each graduate degree is needed, along with a reshaping of the requirements of graduate programs to meet the needs of the professions. In the teaching profession, a greater variety of acceptable degrees and kinds of preparation is needed.

While this section has concentrated on deficiencies in the training of academic subject instructors, Rippey in 1971 stated that the poorest preservice education is received by vocational instructors. In general, faculty training is considered poorer than training for administrators and student service personnel.

Giles in 1971 rated administrator, student service and faculty training as A--, C+ and D, respectively. Harris rated administrator as +,
student services programs as −, and faculty programs, especially "teacher
college" programs, as very −. Moody agrees that non-instructional staff
programs are adequate, perhaps proliferated; "we need programs for
the junior college instructor." Collins believes that universities have had
rather good programs for the training of community-junior college administrators; "all we need is more of them. But when it comes to the preparation of instructors . . . much needs to be done." Collins believes that
much needs to be done with programs for student service workers as
well. Tillery believes that universities have had more difficulty accepting
the need, and providing the training, for community-junior college instructors than for administrators and student service workers (Collins and
Tillery, 1971).

The "Good" Teachers

Many community-junior college faculty do not have the attitudes
and/or the graduate preparation that would aid their adjustment to the
"teaching college." However, there are good community-junior college
instructors. This section attempts to discover and describe their attributes.

Precise knowledge of the influence of college teachers upon student learning and development remains a "vast and significant area that
awaits investigation" (Sanford and Cohen, 1971). There seems little
question that teacher personality is very important in determining success with his students. In a study of 2000 new community-junior college
freshmen, "instructor's personality" was ranked second in a list of eight
"things they look for" when they enter a class for the first time; the
course reading list was ranked last (Cohen and Brawer, 1971).

Blocker (1971) believes that personality is more important than
academic preparation in an instructor's adjustment to the community-
junior college setting. Furthermore, Blocker states that research verifying
his conclusion has been available to universities for twenty years, but
university personnel still haven't absorbed the message.

The personality of the successful college teacher resembles that of
the:

kind of person who has been described by Abraham Maslow as self-actualizing,
by Karen Horney as self-realizing, by Gayle Privette as transcendent-function-
ing, and by Carl Rogers as fully functioning. Other humanistic psychologists
have described such healthy personalities as open to experience, democratic,
accepting, understanding, caring, supporting, approving, loving, nonjudg-
mental. They tolerate ambiguity; their decisions come from within rather than
from without; they have a zest for life, for experiencing, for touching, tasting,

feeling, knowing. They risk involvement; they reach out for experiences; they are not afraid to encounter others or themselves. They believe that man is basically good, and given the right conditions, will move in positive directions. [O'Banion, 1971.]

Combs' studies of good and poor teachers verify O'Banion's general statement. Combs reports that good teachers perceive others as able rather than unable, as friendly instead of unfriendly, as worthy rather than unworthy, as internally motivated rather than externally controlled, as dependable instead of undependable and as helpful rather than obstructive.

Good teachers view themselves differently from poor teachers. Good teachers see themselves as more adequate, trustworthy, and wanted by others than poor teachers. Good teachers operate from internal rather than external frames of reference. They are sensitive to the needs and responses of others and they can communicate this sensitivity (Combs, 1965).

Studies at Michigan and Florida seem to support Combs' findings. At the University of Michigan, McKeachie in 1969 reviewed several studies of successful instructor characteristics. He concluded that successful instructors are able to listen attentively to students, pay attention to general student reactions, be friendly, be permissive and flexible in the classroom, and explain when and why they criticize students. A study of 120 University of Florida students (Lefforge, 1971) indicates that good instructors are identified by students according to their caring, communicating, adapting instruction to students' needs, making goals clear, enthusiasm, knowledge of subject, and developing student self-learning attitudes. The Florida students indicate that poor teachers' worst characteristics are their lack of caring, and demeaning attitudes toward sudents.

Another model of the "self-actualizing" or "healthy" personality is Heath's "reasonable adventurer" (1964). Cohen states that a model group of community-junior college faculty, the "defined-purpose router," resembles the "reasonable adventurer."

The defined-purpose router was developed by Brawer in 1968 as one of four job-orientation models of community-junior college staff. The other categories were end-of-the-roaders, ladder-climbers, and clock-punchers. Of the four categories, only the defined-purpose routers:

. . . are the closest to what one would hope most teachers would become — at all levels of education. They are like Heath's (1964) "reasonable adventurers" — people who have found a reason for being, and who have dedicated themselves to the integration of self and to the attainment of their goals. They see the junior college as a teaching institution, a place where diverse types of students come to seek satisfaction for different needs. They are able to define their subject matter in terms of specific learning objectives, and they help move their students toward a combination of goal-oriented, specified behavior and personality integration. Indeed, because they have found their own sense of identity they are able to project their identity into a professional image. [Cohen, 1971.]

Research on community-junior college instructors seems to agree that the "healthy" personality makes the best teacher. Cohen and Brawer report that community-junior college instructors are rated as good teachers if they have the characteristics of "flexibility" and "feeling." Supervisors give higher ratings to faculty who are considered to be flexible in situations (Cohen, 1971). Teachers are more likely to be employed at community-junior colleges when they indicate preferences on a "feeling" orientation. After several months, "feeling" types are also rated higher by their supervisors than "thinking" types of faculty. Cohen believes that this latter result corroborates Myers and Briggs' contention that "intuitive feeling people . . . may excel in teaching (especially college and high school). . . ."

The good community-junior college instructor "interests and inspires the student to develop himself to the limit of his potential" (Reynolds, 1957). The good instructor's personality may help achieve this task. The flexibility, feelingness, and security of the instructor may help students to develop and maintain their own personal security (Pearce, 1966). A secure personality may also support the good instructor's ability to have an "interest in the student as a person." A flexible and feeling personality may have interest in the student's personal development beyond the classroom.

The effective instructor is able to communicate with students about concerns stretching beyond the classroom; he is also able to communicate subject matter better than the poorer instructor (Garrison, *Approaches,* 1967). Again, his personality helps this communication. Also, his knowledge of the subject matter helps. Skaggs says that the effective community-junior college teacher knows his subject profoundly and in relation to other subjects. Garrison cites a dean's opinion that the effective teacher knows his material so well that he can simplify it without distorting or diluting it.

The good teacher is a scholar of his subject matter, but a scholar whose main goal is the effective communication of his material to students — not communication to professional colleagues only. He is not interested in the idle acquisition of content for his personal use only. Boast (1971) says that three major types of faculty — the high school teacher, the university Ph.D., and the industry/business dropout — can assure community-junior colleges of their possession of content information, "but this has relatively little to do with their being effective teachers in the community college. . . . These people come to us 'content oriented' and not 'people oriented' and 'process oriented,' both of which we need."

The community-junior college teacher's interest in content is valid only as it is also an interest in the communication of content to student. This valid interest marks the good teacher in the two-year college.

Staff Member, 1980s

In 1980, community-junior colleges may employ 78,889–118,000 more staff than in 1971. It is hoped that the colleges will employ more staff who share many of the attributes of 1971's good teachers — communication-orientation to the study of subject matter, flexibility, "feeling," a high regard for students and their total development, — rather than the attributes of many other community-junior college faculty today — an affiliation research-specialization orientation to content, a high affiliation with four-year college standards of education and, sometimes, a low affiliation with two-year college students.

The attributes of good teachers are important for all two-year college staff members regardless of their professional roles. Administrators, library and student services staff members should have personalities and professional orientations which assist their communication with students, colleagues, and others in regard to the development of the goals and programs of the "people's college."

This section attempts to describe further the potential community-junior college staff member of 1980, concentrating on the faculty member, because his development is crucial to the success of the "teaching college."

This section includes also suggestions for the general preparation of a 1980 community-junior college staff. Studies indicate that preparation must be different from what it is today if community-junior college staff attitudes are to come into focus with the purposes and programs of the college. This generalization is especially true for academic subject faculty in the two-year college.

The need for change in present teacher preparation extends beyond the two-year college. This report has already mentioned the Task Force on Higher Education's concern for change in the education of all college and university teachers. The need for reform in public school teacher preparation is cited by Silberman (1970), who says: "there is probably no aspect of contemporary education on which there is greater unanimity of opinion than that teacher education needs a vast overhaul. Virtually everyone is dissatisfied with the current state of teacher education . . ."

These concerns for college and school teacher education reform affect the two-year college since many of its faculty come from college or secondary school teaching positions. Improvement in teacher preparation for other institutional positions would help when and if those teachers come to the "teaching college." But still, even if the preparation of all other teachers were adequate, the need would exist for the reform of two-year college teacher preparation.

While this section makes general suggestions for staff characteristics, faculty especially, it does not suggest that all staff should be the same. There is not, neither should there be, any stereotypical community-junior college teacher, just as there is no "typical" community-junior college student (Medsker, 1964). Many studies indicate that different types of students learn better from different types of faculty, for example, Heath, in 1964. Thus, until future research uncovers more fully how different teachers affect different students, the maintenance of the heterogeneity of two-year college faculty seems advisable. This heterogeneity would undoubtedly be maintained regardless of the following suggestions, but an indication of the intent of the suggestions does not seem inappropriate.

The Humanistic Teacher

The first characteristic of a 1980 staff member focuses on personality. Research has shown that the effective teacher's personality is secure and open to others. It is, in short, a "humanistic" personality . . . it cares for man before thing; it is the personality of the learner who helps others to learn.

The key to the humanistic personality is not its performance of X, Y, Z functions which label the teacher as "humanistic." Rather, the key is the teacher's ability for self-awareness during the performance of any functions. As Jerome Bruner says, it is not what the teacher does but what he is that makes him a good teacher. And the key to what he is is his ability to know himself.

"Know Thyself" was the credo of Socrates, an exemplar for all teachers. Through self-knowledge, the teacher can be himself, and thus, finally, he can *be* with others. That he will act differently with others — respond to others in a style different from other "humanistic" teachers — is assumed. But by being aware of his true "style" with others, 1980's community-junior college teacher will be more able to help others to develop their individual "styles."

April O'Connell describes the humanization of education as simply and as well as it has ever been described:

Education occurs when there is a meeting of persons. If education is a meeting between persons, it follows that the teacher must be a person, not a machine who gives information, not a tyrant who reigns supreme in his own classroom, not a permissive nonentity who provides no challenge and encounter, not an insecure and frightened animal who hides behind academic rigor and discipline lest others view his weaknesses, and not a carbon copy of some earlier teacher or professor who influenced him. [O'Banion, 1971.]

The development of humanistic community-junior college teachers depends largely upon the exposure of these teachers to humanistic models in a humanistic atmosphere — either in graduate school or at the community-junior college. Patterson says that "the importance of a humanistic atmosphere in teacher education is emphasized. It is essential that the education of teachers should be an example of what is being taught (1971)." Thurston (1971) feels that "catalysts" are needed to help develop an atmosphere of respect and stimulation in the community-junior college. The humanization of faculty, Thurston says, works "only in a total institutional climate which is characterized by trust, respect, and a deep concern for people."

The primary purpose of community-junior college staff preparation programs should be the development of staff self-knowledge. This purpose is attained when the program provides:

human, communicative interaction between real persons — student and student, student and faculty, faculty and student; and through such interaction, focuses on the real problems — personal and emotional as well as intellectual and professional — which confront the student in his work. . . . [Rogers, 1969.]

Orientation to the Community-Junior College

The next major purpose of staff preparation programs is to develop the staff's knowledge of the community-junior college environment. This environment includes the college, its philosophy and roles, and the students.

Cosand (1968) believes that 1980s community-junior college "will employ only those who believe wholeheartedly in the philosophy of the community college." Indeed, this belief may help the faculty member to be a better teacher. Cohen cites a study of faculty acceptance of the college concept and concludes that the greater the faulty member's belief in the role of the college, the greater his concern for his students (1971).

The attitudes of many faculty indicate that they do not believe in the philosophy of the community-junior college. Kelly and Connolly (1970) indicate that this apparent disbelief is due to the absence of a lucid projection of the institution's role and of the faculty member's role in the institution in most preservice programs. Thus, faculty are often left to define these roles through on-the-job actions and relationships with other faculty — who may be just as knowledgeable of the institution's role and their role in the institution. Thus, possibly, the four-year college orientation of many faculty may be explained and enhanced by the lack of preservice and inservice orientation of faculty to the community-junior college's role and expectations of faculty.

As early as 1949, the American Council on Education suggested that the first preparation need of community-junior college faculty was "a clear conception of the philosophy and background of the institutions, their relationship to the whole educational structure, and especially their place in the community." Twenty years later, the American Association of Junior Colleges stated that the first preservice training need of two-year college instructors was to know "the historical role of the two-year college and its future place in American higher education." (*Pre-Service,* 1969.)

Knowledge of the community-junior college may help the professional advancement of faculty. Wattenbarger (1971) says that:

repeated studies have indicated that faculty members who are considered by junior college people to be most successful are those who have had at least one course or some direct experience with a course which deals specifically with the community college as a part of the total scheme of higher education.

Orientation to the Community-Junior College Student

Along with knowledge of the philosophy, history, and goals of the community-junior college, staff also need an understanding of the nature of the community-junior college student. After all, the key to the instructor's success is his ability to build an educational relationship with his students. As Holland says, "our concern should sometimes be less for professional ability than an ability to relate to the student body. Nothing gets through to the student if there is not some kind of relationship established. This is not just sensitivity training, but a relationship" (A.A.J.C., *Preparing,* 1969).

This relationship may be fostered by an increase of teacher contact with community-junior college students and with studies about those students prior to his employment at the two-year college. Medsker and Tillery (1971) say that an understanding of how students with varying motivational, interest, and ability patterns learn is essential for the success of the two-year college instructor. Soderquist (1971) says that familiarization with the two-year college's role is important, but perhaps the most significant problem of teacher preparation is to come up with teaching solutions to meet "the needs of a vastly diverse student population amid the political and social forces that are present in our society today." The 1949 A.C.E. report and the 1969 A.A.J.C. report agree that an understanding "of the special problems of age groups" and of "the profile, culture, goals and values of the diverse student population" at community-junior colleges is essential.

The greatest lack of understanding and, therefore the greatest need for understanding students may concern the "low-ability" or "marginal-ability" students who often come from "disadvantaged" backgrounds and, often, enroll in vocational-technical programs. Berg said in 1968:

> There is a large and increasing volume of information concerned with the characteristics, needs, and problems of disadvantaged students and with methods and techniques which seem to have promise of increasing the achievement of such students. In general, educators demonstrate only a limited familiarity with, and understanding of such information. There appears to be little effort to raise that level of familiarity and understanding. Very few junior colleges have established informal or formal in-service training programs for instructors involved in special programs for disadvantaged students or for the administrators and faculty as a whole.

Greco (1971) indicates that the vocational instructors in technical colleges need a more "thorough understanding and appreciation of technical college students, their characteristics, needs and aspirations." His advice may be equally applicable to the vocational-technical students and instructors in "comprehensive" community-junior colleges.

In addition to attempts to inform faculty and other staff about the specific nature of community-junior college students, other attempts might be made which inform faculty indirectly about students. Cosand (1968) feels that 1980's faculty and staff must understand the socioeconomic backgrounds and pressures which affect two-year college students. Thus, an understanding of sociology — especially urban sociology — might help the two-year college teacher to be more effective with students. Also, Patterson indicates that a major defect in teacher preparation is that prospective faculty are not provided with a systematic approach to human behavior (1971). Possibly, courses in developmental psychology and adolescent psychology would help eliminate this defect. Garrison (*Issues,* 1967) says that many community-junior college teachers desire a "good course in adolescent psychology — one dealing frankly and directly with the problems we meet on campuses like these."

The Ability to Teach

The prospective community-junior college faculty member must know himself and he must know his environment — the college and its students. He must also know how to teach his subject matter to his students.

Wattenbarger cites the ability to teach as a qualification for a junior college appointment. This is particularly applicable to the junior college, inasmuch as it professes to be a "teaching" institution (with research and publishing being secondary — or even neglected — activities). Hence the problem confronting the junior college faculty recruiter is compounded not only by the task of seeking sufficient numbers of properly certified teachers, but also the difficulty of finding an ample number of *competent* (if not gifted) teachers. [Gaddy, 1969.]

At first, the ability to teach seems to be needed only by faculty in the community-junior college. Yet, the teaching emphasis in the community-junior college is on the communication of any potentially educating subject matter to students. Therefore, the counselor, librarian, or administrator could profit from preparation in this area of teaching-communication skills.

The concern about instructor teaching ability is as old as the community-junior college itself. The 1949 A.C.E. report recommended an instructor with "adequate skill in curriculum construction, evaluation, and other areas related to the art and science of instruction in these institutions." In a 1957 Florida conference, Reynolds said that a characteristic of the effective teacher was command of communication skills; this characteristic was so obvious that Reynolds doubted that he should even have mentioned it. At the same conference, however, Skaggs mentioned it. He said that teachers needed to know the skills, procedures, and methods of good instruction. They also needed to know learning theories and methods of evaluation of students. Finally, in 1969, the A.A.J.C. brochure on *Pre-Service Training of Two-Year College Instructors* mentioned six areas of improvement of instruction. These areas could be classified into three main groups: evaluation; teaching techniques and media aids; and subject matter development.

Evaluation

The community-junior college staff member of the 1980s should be aware of two major areas of evaluation — behavioral objectives, and testing and measurement. A general need for the evaluation of instruction was cited by the American Council on Education in 1949. But in the past few years the need for evaluation, or accountability, has been a dominant theme in the community-junior college. In 1971, the theme of the American Association of Junior Colleges' annual convention was "accountability and the two-year college." The March, 1971, title of the *Junior College Journal* consisted of one word, "Accountability."

What the school boards and the public call "accountability" is actually an old student question — What are we supposed to learn? — with a new twist — How do we know that we have learned it? Nordh (1971) adds that accountability means that educators, especially administrators and faculty members, are responsible for student learning. Community-junior college faculty and administrators are especially responsible because their colleges have evolved as a result of public pressures for better education.

The chief means of accountability has been the behavioral objective — the specific goal for student learning or staff member performance which is expected to be accomplished by the student or staff member. Several community-junior colleges have begun to organize their entire structures around the behavioral objective concept, e.g., Brookdale Community College in New Jersey and William Rainey Harper College in Illinois.

Behavioral objectives can be evaluation devices for faculty, student service staff or administrators. However, the crux of the success for which the "teaching college" will be held accountable lies in faculty-student cooperation in the creation of learning objectives.

The University of Florida study indicates to some degree that good teachers make goals clear for students (Lefforge, 1971). Cohen and Brawer state that "apparently, teachers must be very clear about their objectives and, further, must develop those aspects of their natural styles that best lead students to attain those objectives" (1971). Cohen (1969) goes on to say that those teachers who do not clearly specify student performance standards and still judge student performance are not just poor teachers; they are immoral, because "judgments on the basis of nebulous or shifting criteria are the ultimate immorality."

Johnson (1971) states that the definition of instructional objectives emerged as a thematic emphasis in the development of curriculum, instructional improvement, and general instructional innovation in his recent survey of community-junior college innovation. He indicates that these objectives helped to launch several total institution "system approaches" to instruction.

Thus, the community-junior college may be beginning a journey toward total institutional involvement in the evaluation of student learning. By 1980, that journey may have progressed to the point where administrators, student service personnel and instructors who are unfamiliar with the formation and evaluation of objectives, may be left behind.

Another aspect of evaluation is testing and measurement. A major need for faculty education in this area was cited by the community-junior college administrators in the A.A.J.C.'s In-Service training survey. Perhaps here, the education of student services personnel, especially counselors, could serve as a model for the preparation of instructional faculty. Most counselors have taken specific courses in testing and measurement as part of their master's degree programs.

Teaching Techniques and Media Aids

Most community college instructors, like those at the secondary and higher education levels, spend much time on subject matter and little on teaching techniques. It is paradoxical that many instructors, expert in fields that have made rapid strides in the past ten or twenty years, are still using teaching techniques that were used hundreds and even thousands of years ago. It is even stranger that they lack any desire to find new ways of teaching. They rely automatically on the lecture as the sole means of transmitting knowledge from one generation to the next. [Banister, 1970.]

One instructor said, "If we were to be ruthlessly honest with ourselves, we would admit we are teaching the same old stuff in the same old way. Standard textbooks, students sitting in front of us in rows, papers, quizzes, and all of the traditional apparatus. A lot of us would like to try some innovations. But we are not sure how to go about it. We usually don't have enough time to try it. And frankly, we don't know where to turn for help." [Garrison, *Issues,* 1967.]

These colleges will realize in 1980, I hope and believe, that there are many methods of teaching and that each teacher may have a method which is best for him. An administrator will not demand that all teachers teach in the same way, but that they make use of every accessible and appropriate teaching aid: slides, computers, tape recorders and many other audiovisual materials. [Cosand, 1968.]

"There is a better way to teach — a better course — a better curriculum. There must be a better way, if we are to succeed." These are the words of Cosand's (1968) "new breed of teachers and administrators" in community-junior colleges. The words indicate that the "teaching college's" success will depend largely upon the development of faculty and administrator's "knowledge of modern media and new techniques of instruction" (Medsker and Tillery, 1971).

Johnson lists programmed instruction, technological aids to learning, special facilities for large group instruction, students as teachers, work-study programs, and sensitivity training and encounter groups among 1971's innovative techniques for community-junior college instruction (1971). Faculty preparation in programmed instruction is a specific recommendation of the administrators in the A.A.J.C. survey. The President's Task Force on Higher Education (1970) believes that there are unresolved questions regarding the validity of traditional large-class lectures and the optimum use of mechanically aided teaching and learning, including audiovisual, television, and computer-aided instruction. Perhaps some of those questions could be answered by community-junior college faculty preparation in the use of new teaching techniques and media aids. Perhaps then, "the size of the class [would] not necessarily determine the presence or lack of personal attention — the teaching methods [would be] the determining factors (Cosand, 1968).

The use of new teaching methods and media aids should become a major focus of the preparation of faculty who participate in remedial and disadvantaged student education programs. For many reasons, remedial and disadvantaged students have not been helped by traditional methods of education. "Outstanding, innovative, fresh and dynamic" instructional techniques are needed to teach these students (Moore, 1970). Soderquist (1971) believes that the development of these new teaching methods for remedial programs deserves special attention in the preparation of community-junior college faculty.

Subject-Matter Development

The A.A.J.C. statement on preservice training mentions that community-junior college faculty should be aware of the theory and techniques of curriculum development. More specifically, teachers should help develop "core subjects" on an interdisciplinary approach to the subject matter. The A.C.E. recommends that instructors be skilled in curriculum construction. In 1949, the A.C.E. proposed the specific development of ´a new curricular approach to subject matter — broad functionalist development relating subject matter to the practical problems of the local community.

The development of new course content has been a traditional suggestion in community-junior colleges. But the reality still is, too often, traditional course content which reflects the teacher's experiences in education from grammar school to graduate school. As has been shown previously, this content and these experiences may actually hinder student learning in community-junior colleges.

Garrison (1971) believes that the community-junior college faculty member's:

Typical graduate preparation is too narrowly subject-oriented, specialty-oriented: not eclectic enough, not cross-disciplinary enough, and — frankly — not intellectually rigorous enough to produce tough-minded and flexible instructors. It pays too little attention to the process of learning a subject, and too much attention to the merely accumulative aspect of information.

If this form of education fails to produce "toughminded and flexible instructors," then it seems very unlikely that this form of education will produce toughminded and flexible community-junior college students.

The community-junior college teacher should receive rigorous graduate preparation in his major subject field (A.A.J.C., *Pre-Service,* 1969) but this preparation should be re-thought and recast with new goals in mind (Garrison, 1967). The primary goal is to bend the subject matter to the student rather than the student to the subject matter. Subject matter should be a servant, not a master of student learning; an instrument, not an end (Moore, 1970).

The community-junior college student is a freshman or sophomore. He needs course content which is general and appropriate to his learning needs. Garrison [*Issues,* 1967] says that many instructors desire "broad, solid, general (graduate) courses, full of the kind of material that we are going to teach." Garrison states that "instructors (are) not suggesting watered-down versions of regular lower division courses. Rather they [are] groping for help in designing fresh and more effective ways to handle the level of material with the varied student groups, especially in community colleges."

Community-junior college students do not need hyperspecialized education at the freshman or sophomore level. Rather, they need general education. This general education may be in a particular subject area, but it should also include references to related subject areas. In other words, interdisciplinary education should be a part of the educational experience of two-year college students and the graduate preparation of two-year college faculty.

The A.A.J.C. recommendation for development of interdisciplinary education has been mentioned previously. If "discipline" is regarded as a flexible term, then the A.C.E. recommendation is also a call for interdisciplinary education in two-year colleges.

Cosand has stated that 1980's faculty will seek freedom from traditional barriers of departmental structure and one-discipline courses.

The isolation of the subject-matter specialist will be a thing of the past in the community college of tomorrow and, I hope, in all of higher education. The English teacher will be concerned with the students in technical education, the philosophy teacher with the physical-education major, the artist with the retailing student, and the mathematics instructor with the musician. A faculty should be a whole. All must work together in mutual respect if all their responsibilities are to be fulfilled. [1968.]

Administrators and student service personnel will also be involved in this interdisciplinary mutuality. Already in 1971, colleges are being organized on the basis of interdisciplinary clusters of teachers, student services personnel and administrators, e.g. Santa Fe Junior College in Florida and the College of DuPage in Illinois. These clusters transcend the traditional departmentalized college structure in order to focus on student learning rather than subject teaching.

Summary

In this section of the report the characteristics of the community-junior college staff member are described. The "typical" community-junior college faculty member is a 31–50 year old middle-class white male whose previous work experience has been in the public schools or in business and industry. He has a master's degree in his subject area. His coursework has been taken at four-year institutions and has seldom included the study of the community-junior college. Many of these instructors are steeped in traditional academic processes and prefer to work in four-year colleges and universities. Many do not support basic tenets of community-junior college philosophy, and may have great distaste for a significant proportion of students who attend these institutions.

Graduate education as it presently exists does not help alleviate these concerns. Indeed, as presently constructed, graduate education probably fosters attitudes that are the antithesis of the "good" community-junior college instructor.

Characteristics of the good teacher for the community-junior college are then described. The good teacher is humanistic and knowledgeable. He is both warm-hearted and hard-headed. Briefly, program needs for the preparation of such faculty members are outlined.

The staff member of 1970 is rapidly moving toward the ideal characteristics posited for the staff member of 1980. Effective programs of preservice and inservice education will insure that more staff members will reflect the ideal in 1980 than do in 1970.

References

American Association of Junior Colleges. *In-Service Training for Two-Year College Faculty and Staff*. Washington, D.C., August 21, 1969.

————. *Preservice Training of Two-Year College Instructors*. Washington, D.C., 1969.

————. *Preserving Training of Two-Year College Instructors*. Washington, D.C., 1969.

————. *To Work in a Junior College*. Washington, D.C., 1966.

American Council on Education. *Wanted: 30,000 Instructors for Community Colleges*. Washington, D.C., 1949.

Anderson, E. F. and Spencer, J. D. *Report of Selected Data and Characteristics of Illinois Public Junior Colleges: 1966–67.* Springfield, Illinois: Illinois Junior College Board, 1967.

——————. *Report of Selected Data and Characteristics of Illinois Public Junior Colleges: 1967–68.* Springfield, Illinois: Illinois Junior College Board, 1968.

—————— and Thornblad, C. E. *Report of Selected Data and Characteristics of Illinois Public Junior Colleges: 1968–69.* Springfield, Illinois: Illinois Junior College Board, 1969.

Anthony, J. Vice President, College of DuPage. Letter, November 12, 1971.

Banister, R. *Case Studies in Multi-Media Instruction.* ERIC Clearinghouse for Junior Colleges, Topical Paper No. 13. Los Angeles: University of California, 1970.

Beazley, R. *Numbers and Characteristics of Employees in Institutions of Higher Education: Fall 1966.* Washington, D.C.: National Center for Educational Statistics, 1970.

——————. *Numbers and Characteristics of Employees in Institutions of Higher Education: Fall 1967.* Washington, D.C.: National Center for Educational Statistics, 1971.

Berg, E. H. and Axtell, D. *Programs for Disadvantaged Students in the California Community Colleges.* Oakland, California: Peralta Junior College District, 1968.

Blake, L. President, Flathead Valley Community College. Letter, October 26, 1971.

Blocker, C. E. President, Harrisburg Area Community College. Letter, October 28, 1971.

Boast, W. Dean General Studies, Community College of Denver, West Campus. Letter, October 28, 1971.

Brawer, F. B. *Personality Characteristics of College and University Faculty: Implications for the Community College.* ERIC Clearinghouse for Junior Colleges, Monograph 3. Washington, D.C.: American Association of Junior Colleges, 1968.

Buber, M. *Israel and the World: Essays in a Time of Crisis.* New York: Schocken Books, 1948.

Carnegie Commission on Higher Education. *The Open-Door Colleges.* New York: McGraw-Hill Book Company, 1970.

Chronister, J. L. *In-Service Training for Two-Year College Faculty and Staff: The Role of the Graduate Institutions.* Charlottesville, Virginia: University of Virginia, 1970.

Cohen, A. M. *Dateline '79: Heretical Concepts for the Community College.* Beverly Hills, California: Glencoe Press, 1969.

——————, and Associates. *A Constant Variable.* San Francisco: Jossey-Bass Inc., 1971.

——————, and Brawer, F. B. *The Dynamic Interaction of Student and Teacher.* ERIC Clearinghouse for Junior Colleges, Topical Paper No. 17. Los Angeles: University of California, 1971.

Collins, C. and Tillery, D. Interview. San Francisco: November 4, 1971.

Combs, A. W. *The Professional Education of Teachers: A Perceptual View of Teacher Education.* Boston: Allyn and Bacon, 1965.

————, Avila, D. L. and Purkey, W. W. *Helping Relationships: Basic Concepts for the Helping Professions.* Boston: Allyn and Bacon, 1971.

Cosand, J. "The Community College in 1980" in *Campus 1980.* New York: Dell Publishing Co., 1968. 134–149.

————, Director, Center for the Study of Higher Education, University of Michigan. Letter, November 11, 1971.

Eells, W. C. *The Junior College.* New York: Houghton Mifflin Company, 1931.

Evans, R. "Staff Development in Vocational Education" in *A Seminar on Graduate Education Programs.* Columbus, Ohio: Ohio State University, 1970.

Fordyce, J. "The Role of the Junior College in Teacher Education." Mimeographed speech, 1970.

Friedman, N. L. "Career Stages and Organizational Role Decisions of Teachers in Two Public Junior Colleges." *Sociology of Education,* Summer, 1967, 40, 231–245.

Garrison, R. H. Remarks in *Approaches Toward Meeting the Personnel Needs of Junior and Four-Year Colleges.* Washington, D.C.: Division of Graduate Programs, U.S.O.E., 1967.

————. *Junior College Faculty: Issues and Problems.* Washington, D.C.: American Association of Junior Colleges, 1967.

————. Letter, November 1, 1971.

————. "The Making of a College Teacher." Proceedings of the Seventh Annual Meeting of the Council of Graduate Schools in the United States. Washington, D.C.: November 30-December 2, 1967.

————. *Teaching in a Junior College.* Washington, D.C.: American Association of Junior Colleges, 1967.

Giles, F. T. Dean, College of Education, University of Washington. Letter, November 4, 1971.

Gleazer, E. J., Jr. "Preparation of Junior College Teachers." *Educational Record,* Spring 1967, 48, 147–152.

Grady, D. "Faculty Recruitment." *ERIC Junior College Research Review.* Washington, D.C.: American Association of Junior Colleges, September, 1969.

Graybeal, W. S. "Faculty and Administrative Salaries." *Junior College Journal,* Vol. 39, No. 1, September, 1968.

Greco, C. Planning Officer, State Technical Colleges, Connecticut. Letter, October 28, 1971.

Harris, N. C. Coordinator of Community College Development, University of Michigan. Letter, November 8, 1971.

Heath, R. *The Reasonable Adventurer.* Pittsburgh, Pennsylvania: University of Pittsburgh, 1964.

Illinois Junior College Board. *Report of Selected Data and Characteristics of Illinois Public Junior Colleges: 1970–71*. Springfield, Illinois: 1971.

Johnson, B. L. "Superior Instruction: A Must for the Junior College." *A Day at Santa Fe*. Gainesville, Florida: University of Florida Institute of Higher Education, 1971.

Jung, C. G. *The Undiscovered Self*. New York: Mentor Books, 1958.

Kelly, M. F. and Connolly, J. *Orientation for Faculty in Junior College Reading Programs*. ERIC Clearinghouse for Junior Colleges, Topical Paper No. 18. Los Angeles: University of California, 1971.

Kerstiens, G. *Directions for Research and Innovation in Junior College Reading Programs*. ERIC Clearinghouse for Junior Colleges, Topical Paper No. 18. Los Angeles: University of California, 1971.

Lefforge, U. S. *Inservice Training as an Instrument for Change*. Gainesville, Florida: University of Florida, Institute of Higher Education, 1971.

Lehrman, E. State Director, Wisconsin Board of Vocational, Technical and Adult Education. Letter, November 2, 1971.

Litton, M. L. Professor of Higher Education, Florida State University. Letter, October 27, 1971.

Mallan, J. P. Director of AAJC Program for Servicemen and Veterans. Memorandum to T. O'Banion, November 11, 1971.

Martin, A. H. and Thornblad, C. E. *Report of Selected Data and Characteristics of Illinois Public Junior Colleges: 1969–70*. Springfield, Illinois: Illinois Junior College Board, 1970.

McKeachie, W. J. *Teaching Tips: A Guidebook for the Beginning College Teacher*. Lexington: D.C. Heath and Co., 1969.

Medsker, L. *The Junior College: Progress and Prospect*. New York: McGraw-Hill, 1960.

————. "The Junior College Student." Mimeographed paper, 1964.

———— and Tillery, H. *Breaking the Access Barriers: A Profile of Two-Year Colleges*. New York: McGraw-Hill, 1971.

Montagu, A. *On Being Human*. New York: Hawthorn Books, Inc., 1966.

Moody, G. V. Director, Division of Junior Colleges, Department of Education, State of Mississippi. Letter, November 3, 1971.

Moore, W. *Against the Odds*. San Francisco: Jossey-Bass Inc., Publishers, 1970.

National Education Association. "Salaries in Higher Education 1967–68." Research report, 1968.

National Science Foundation. *The Junior College and Education in the Sciences*. Washington, D.C.: 1967.

Newman, F. *Report on Higher Education*. Washington, D.C.: U.S. Department of Health, Education, and Welfare, 1971.

Nordh, D. M. "Accountability and the Community College." *Junior College Journal*, 41, March, 1971.

O'Banion, T. U. "Humanizing Education in the Community College." *The Journal of Higher Education*, XLII, November, 1971.

Parker, G. G. *The Enrollment Explosion.* New York: School and Society Books, 1971.

Patterson, C. H. "The Preparation of Humanistic Teachers." Mimeographed paper, 1971.

Pearce, F. C. *Basic Education of Teachers: Seven Needed Qualities.* Modesto, California: Modesto Junior College, 1966.

Phair, T. S. "New Full-Time Faculty Members Selected by California Community Colleges for the 1970–71 Academic Year." Unpublished paper. Fall 1970.

Reynolds, J. P. "The Academic Instructors." *Teachers for the Community Colleges of Florida.* Tallahassee: Florida State University, 1957.

Rice, L. H. Assistant Dean, Graduate School, Idaho State University. Letter, October 29, 1971.

Rippey, D. President, El Centro College. Letter, October 29, 1971.

Rogers, C. R. *Freedom to Learn.* Columbus, Ohio: Charles Merrill Publishing Company, 1969.

Siehr, H. E.; Jamrich, J. X.; and Hereford, K. T. *Problems of New Faculty Members in Community Colleges.* East Lansing, Michigan: American Association of Junior Colleges, 1963.

Silberman, C. E. *Crisis in the Classroom.* New York: Random House, 1970.

Simon, K. A. and Grant, W. V. *Digest of Educational Statistics: 1968 Edition.* Washington, D.C.: National Center for Educational Statistics, 1968.

Singer, D. S. "Do We Need a Community College Institute?" *Junior College Journal,* Vol. 39, No. 2, October 1968.

Skaggs, K. G. "The Qualifications of the Good Junior College Teacher." *Teachers for the Community Colleges of Florida.* Tallahassee: Florida State University, 1957.

Soderquist, W. E. Assistant to the President, Southwest College. Letter, October 20, 1971.

Thornton, J. W. *The Community-Junior College.* John Wiley and Sons, 1960.

Thurston, A. President, Garland College. Letter, November 1, 1971.

United States President's Task Force on Higher Education. *Priorities in Higher Education.* Washington, D.C.: U.S. Government Printing Office, 1970.

Wattenbarger, J. L. "Staffing the Community Colleges: Who, Where, Why, and How?" *Junior College Staffing 1975–80.* Normal, Illinois: Illinois State University, 1971.

5. Projection of Staff Needs

The 1960s have been called the boom period of community-junior college development because of the vast increase of student and institution numbers. Student enrollment increased from 748,619 in 1960–61 to 2,186,272 in 1969–70. (Table 5.1) Institutions opened at the approximate rate of one per week; by the end of the boom period, they had increased their numbers by two-thirds.

However, the boom growth affected only one sector of community-junior colleges, the public; the private sector's student and staff size increased only slightly while the number of private colleges decreased. Public community-junior college student and staff size more than tripled during the 1960s; the number of colleges doubled (Tables 5.1, 5.2).

By 1970, private community-junior colleges played a diminishing role in the education of the nation's two-year college students. While in 1964 they had 11.4 percent of all two-year students, in 1970 the percentage dropped to 5.4. The percentage of staff members dropped from 17.2 percent to 8.6 percent during the same period.

During the growth years of the 1960s, the ratio of instructional staff to administrative and professional service staff, (counselors, librarians, et al), remained stable. Public colleges maintained a 9:1 ratio and private colleges maintained a 7:2.8 ratio.

The ratio of instructors to students showed a slight increase at public colleges and a slight decrease at private colleges. The public college ratio moved from 1:20.83 in 1961 to 1:22.53 in 1970. The private college ratio changed from 1:15.25 to 1:14.7 during the same period.

Projection of Needs

The following projections of community-junior college staff needs are based on student enrollment. The Carnegie Commission has computed

TABLE 5.1

**Community-Junior Colleges: Students and Institutions
1961–1970 (AAJC, Directories, 1966–71)**

	Number of Colleges		
Year	Public	Private	Total
1961	405	273	678
1962	426	278	704
1963	422	272	694
1964	452	267	719
1965	503	268	771
1966	565	272	837
1967	648	264	912
1968	739	254	993
1969	794	244	1038
1970	847	244	1091

	Students		
Year	Public	Private	Total
1961	644,968	103,651	748,619
1962	713,334	105,535	818,869
1963	814,244	113,290	927,534
1964	921,093	122,870	1,043,963
1965	1,152,086	140,667	1,292,753
1966	1,316,980	147,119	1,464,099
1967	1,528,220	143,220	1,671,440
1968	1,810,964	143,152	1,954,116
1969	2,051,493	134,779	2,186,272
1970	2,366,028	133,809	2,499,837

three possible two-year college student enrollment projections for 1980. Projection A assumes that the proportion of all college undergraduates in community-junior colleges will remain at the 1968 level, 29 percent. Projection B assumes that community-junior colleges will receive 60 percent of the increase of all undergraduate enrollment after 1968. Projection C is based on a per state average community-junior college enrollment, which becomes about a 6 percent national increase by 1980 [1970, 33–34].

In terms of total student numbers, the 1980 two-year college enrollments equal:

Projection A — 3,100,000
Projection B — 4,430,000
Projection C — 3,740,000

By 1970, projection A had been surpassed in several states and projection B was considered realistic only for a few states — e.g., California, Illinois, Florida — where community-junior colleges already had a major

TABLE 5.2

Community-Junior Colleges: Professional Staff
1960–61 to 1970–71 (NCES, 1971, 71–72)

| | Public | | |
Year	Instructors Staff	Other Staff	Total Staff
1960–61	29,000	3,000	32,000
1961–62	30,966	3,416	34,382
1962–63	34,000	4,000	38,000
1963–64	37,365	4,097	41,462
1964–65	43,000	5,000	48,000
1965–66	53,000	6,000	58,000
1966–67	62,000	7,000	69,000
1967–68	74,000	8,000	82,000
1968–69	90,000	10,000	99,000
1969–70	99,000	11,000	110,000
1970–71	105,000	11,000	117,000

| | Private | | |
Year	Instructors Staff	Staff Other	Total Staff
1960–61	6,800	2,500	9,300
1961–62	6,795	2,600	9.400
1962–63	7,500	2,900	10,400
1963–64	7,675	3,077	10,752
1964–65	9,400	3,800	13,200
1965–66	10,900	4,400	15,200
1966–67	11,100	4,500	15,500
1967–68	10,100	4,100	14,200
1968–69	10,500	4,200	14,800
1969–70	8,800	3,600	12,400
1970–71	9,100	3,700	12,800

portion of the total undergraduate enrollment. Therefore, for most states, C was considered the most realistic projection of student enrollment.

In 1971, Medsker and Tillery, derived two faculty-student ratios from projection C — 1:25 and 1:20. The first ratio was based on an increase of students to faculty because of technological improvements and curricular innovations. The second ratio was based on a decline and eventual stabilization of the faculty to student ratio. [1971, 100]. From these two ratios Medsker and Tillery projected a need for 71,000–89,000 new and replacement community-junior college faculty by 1980 [1971, 101].

The National Center for Educational Statistics has projected community-junior college faculty needs on the basis of straight line enrollment rates over the past eleven years and total population estimates for

1971–80. The Center predicts that 72,000 new community-junior college faculty will be needed by 1980 [1971, 72].

However, the N.C.E.S. statistics do not account for replacement faculty. Replacement faculty are hired as a result of present faculty separations, retirements, or death. Medsker and Tillery estimate that 24,000–30,000 such faculty will be needed in community-junior colleges by 1980 [1971, 101]. When Medsker and Tillery's upper approximation of replacement faculty is added to the N.C.E.S. figure, the total prediction jumps to 102,000 new and replacement faculty for community-junior colleges in 1980.

The projection of administrative and service staff needs has been difficult for some community-junior college researchers. In 1965, Schultz predicted a need for 82.2 new chief administrators per annum until 1970 [1965]. However, in 1968, Schultz declared that his yearly estimate had been nearly doubled in 1966 and 1967 because of an unforeseen increase in the numbers of new two-year colleges throughout the nation [1968].

The National Center for Educational Statistics has computed a need for 9,500 new full-time and part-time administrative and service staff by 1980. But this figure may be conservative for two reasons: like Schultz's predictions, it does not account for new colleges; and again, the figure does not account for replacement staff needs. The Carnegie Commission believes that 230–280 new community-junior colleges should be established by 1980 [1970, 1]. At a conceivable rate of 15 administrative and service positions per new college, a total of 3,500 new personnel may be needed. Replacement staff may total about 3,000 if the present public college faculty-administration ratio remains constant, and if Medsker and Tillery's projected number of replacement faculty is correct. Thus, when these new and replacement figures are added to the 9,500 computed by N.C.E.S. some 16,000 new administrative and service staff may be needed in community-junior colleges by 1980.

A much more conservative figure is gained from Medsker and Tillery's prediction that 71,000–89,000 new faculty will be needed in community-junior colleges in 1980. Taking 1/9 of that figure, (the ratio of administrative and service staff to instructional staff in public two-year colleges), the administrative and service staff needs become 7,889–9,867 new and replacement personnel.

In summary then, 1980's community-junior colleges should include 3,100,000 to 4,430,000 students with 3,740,000 students as the most likely size. The instructional staff should number between 185,100 and 216,100, an increase of 71,000–102,000 new and replacement faculty. Administrative and service personnel should increase by 7,889–16,000 for a total of 22,589–30,700 of these staff members.

References

American Association of Junior Colleges. *1966–1971 Junior College Directories.* Washington, D.C.: 1966–1971.

Carnegie Commission on Higher Education. *The Open-Door Colleges.* New York: McGraw-Hill Book Company, June, 1970.

Medsker, L. and Tillery, D. *Breaking the Access Barrier: A Profile of Two-Year Colleges.* New York: McGraw-Hill Book Company, 1971.

National Center for Educational Statistics. *Projection of Educational Statistics to 1979–80.* Washington, D.C.: 1971.

Schultz, R. E. *Administrators for America's Junior Colleges: Predictions of Needs, 1965–80.* Washington, D.C.: American Association of Junior Colleges, 1965.

————. "The Junior College President: Who and Where From?" in *The Junior College President.* Los Angeles: American Association of Junior Colleges, 1969.

6. Priorities for the Seventies

There is a set of assumptions contained in this report that can be supported in part by available data and in part by the considered opinion of major spokesmen for the community-junior college. These assumptions are as follows:

(1) Community-junior colleges are special kinds of educational institutions, in some ways similar to, but in some important ways vastly different from, secondary schools and four-year colleges and universities.

(2) Community-junior college students are special kinds of students, similar to their counterparts in other educational institutions, but significantly different in a wide range of characteristics.

(3) There is great need for the great number of community college staff members who are especially qualified to serve these kinds of students in these kinds of institutions.

(4) If the community-junior college is to grow in quality as it has in quantity; if the needs of minority groups are to be met; if the under-educated are to have a second chance; if the needs of business, industry, and government are to be provided for; if communities are to be given opportunities for renewal and rehabilitation; if all human beings are to be given opportunities to explore, extend, and experience their hopes and dreams; then it is imperative that immediate and considerable attention be given to the educational needs of those who staff "democracy's college." For if the staff fails the college fails. And if this college fails, this democracy will be obliged, out of great travail, to generate other institutions to accomplish the proper work of the community-junior college.

[83]

(5) While there are some promising programs currently available in universities and community-junior colleges, programs for preservice and inservice education are mostly nonexistent or inappropriate where they do exist.

(6) Imaginative and potent educational programs for community-junior college staff, supported by the federal government, state and local governments, four-year colleges and universities, community-junior colleges, private foundations, and other appropriate agencies, must be continued where they exist and organized and developed where they do not, if the community college concept is to survive at all much less grow and mature in its contributions to American society.

This section of the report recommends priorities and describes actions for the 1970s, the decade in which educational institutions will be challenged to meet social needs as they have never been challenged before in any period of human history.

Preservice vs. Inservice Programs

With very few exceptions, preservice programs for the preparation of community-junior college staff are grossly inadequate. The disciplines in the university are inflexible; the colleges of education are unsure and unpracticed. Available instructors are either discipline-oriented, narrow, subject-matter specialists or secondary school-oriented, college of education graduates. Neither is prepared to instruct at the community-junior college.

Community-junior college administrators are outspoken in their criticism regarding preservice programs:

There are practically no strong preservice collegiate programs for community college staff members, and those that are in operation provide only a small fraction of the *qualified* personnel needed. Increasing numbers of so-called preservice programs have been established but they are too often only 'blisters' on School of Education programs and are generally inadequate or worse than nothing. [Joseph Cosand, Former President, St. Louis Junior College District, Missouri.]

Preservice college and university programs are generally inadequate to our needs, principally for lack of concern with instructional purposes, learning, and organization for instruction. [Robert McCabe, Executive Vice President, Miami-Dade Junior College, Florida.]

In direct answer to the question how adequate are university preparation programs, I would reply that with few exceptions they missed the mark. [Clyde Blocker, President, Harrisburg Area Community College, Pennsylvania.]

The situation is so intolerable that some critics have suggested that universities should not even attempt to prepare community-junior college staff. These critics have recommended that all available energies and funds should be channeled into programs of inservice education to be coordinated by the community-junior colleges.

It is academic, however, to argue whether universities should prepare staff for the community-junior college. The fact is that universities do prepare staff and will continue to do so. In the 1970s, funds are needed to continue the outstanding programs, to upgrade the inadequate programs, and to develop new programs — programs specifically designed for the preparation of community-junior college personnel.

Even if a variety of continuing and new graduate programs are available in this decade, however, the needs of the community-junior college will be only partially met. In the 1970s, the majority of new staff for the community-junior college will come from business and industry, elementary and secondary schools, other community-junior colleges, and graduate programs that are not designed for this level of education. These staff members, along with the vast majority of staff members currently employed, will need extensive inservice educational opportunities if they are to realize their potential for the institutions in which they work. It is recommended, therefore, that the highest priority be given to the funding of inservice programs.

This is not to suggest that preservice programs should not have high priority. On the contrary, it is extremely important that these programs be adequately supported to insure that the new, ever increasing numbers of community-junior college staff will not have to encounter the time-consuming and expensive limitations of re-education programs.

Too, preservice programs are seldom that only; most university programs are complementary and offer pre- and inservice opportunities. Adequate support for preservice programs will also provide support for university-developed inservice programs.

Preservice Programs

Dimensions of Programs for Community-Junior College Staff

Although the American Association of Junior Colleges estimates that there are approximately 100 graduate institutions offering programs that include the preparation of community-junior college faculty, there is little evidence to suggest that these programs are adequate for the task. Too often a single course is titled "The Junior College," and this course is the total experience of those who graduate from these "specialized" programs. The English instructor takes the same sequence of literature courses as the Ph.D. candidate — and a course in "The Junior College." The counselor takes the same sequence of counseling psychology — and a course in "The Junior College." The administrator takes the same sequence of courses as the secondary school principal or the Ph.D. candidate in higher education — and a course in "The Junior College." What is more ludicrous, the course on "The Junior College" is often taught by a professor who has had no experience in and who has little understanding of the community-junior college.

The first qualities which a preservice program must generate are an understanding of the history and a commitment to the philosophy of the community junior college. Staff members must have knowledge of and appreciation for characteristics common to this institution: open door, community service, teaching oriented, student centeredness, comprehensive curriculum (career programs, developmental programs, general education, continuing education, and transfer programs), etc. While these characteristics are also present in some other American educational systems, they have developed special meaning in the community-junior college; they combine to make this institution unlike any other institution of education in the nation or the world.

The second recommendation is as important as the first. This recommendation is for preservice programs which facilitate staff understanding and acceptance of the students who attend the community-junior college. The diversity of students in age, ability, socioeconomic background, ethnic background, and personality characteristics is greater than in any other institution of higher education. The prospective community-junior staff member must be keenly aware of this diversity, and he must be able to provide a wide range of learning experiences for these students. Above all, he must believe that these students can learn.

In addition to these two basic dimension of a special program, an internship is strongly recommended for all staff members who would work in a community-junior college. For instructors, the internship should be under the supervision of a master teacher at the community-junior level. For counselors and administrators, supervision should be provided by highly competent personnel in these fields. The internship should be a paid experience, and the intern should be a member of the staff — to further his full involvement in the institution. While the university should assist in coordinating the internship program, the primary program responsibility should be given to the community-junior college. The commitment of the community-junior college to the internship program is essential if quality experiences are to be provided to interns. Excellent cooperative intern programs that could serve as models have been developed in several regions.

The length of internship should be sufficient for the prospective staff member's immersion in his potential area of expertise. Most internships should extend for at least a full term (semester, quarter, trimester). Special internships may extend for a full year. In some cases, mini-internships and rotating internships may be appropriate.

An understanding of the philosophy and history of the community-junior college, a knowledge and appreciation of community-junior college students, and an internship are three dimensions which should be included in any program designed to prepare staff for the community-junior college. In addition, instructors must have an understanding of the learning process and be acquainted with new approaches and innovations in learning.

While community-junior colleges have loudly claimed to be "teaching institutions," they might be sadly quiet if they ever examined their true production of student learning. Given the mission of the community-junior college and the challenge of the community-junior college student, the quality of the teaching-learning process is woefully inadequate. Many instructors for these institutions do not know *how* to teach, and they are not helped to know how in most teacher education programs. Present approaches, professor modeling and methodology courses, are primitive and weak. It is hoped that advances in microteaching, systems learning, encounter groups, and other learning technologies will provide improved bases for teacher education programs.

In addition to learning about the process of learning, instructors must be aware of new approaches and innovations in education. Behavioral objectives, multimedia systems, audio-tutorial systems, computer-assisted learning, micro-groups, and many other approaches need to be studied so that instructors can adapt these to their own styles.

So far, this section has sketched minimal requirements for the improvement of graduate preparation programs for community-junior college staff. However, another requirement, the development of the "humanistic" personality, is more important than all the others, for ultimately this personality distinguishes the superior from the inferior educator. The superior "humanistic" educator values human beings. He believes that all human beings can learn; he is deeply committed to the facilitation of human development — on a variety of levels in a variety of ways. His style is to challenge, encourage, support, stimulate, encounter. He is knowledgeable, creative, imaginative, and innovative. He is essential if the community-junior college is to come to full fruition as the "people's college." Therefore, if the "people's college" is to become a reality in the 1970s, the highest support should be given to those graduate programs which develop this "humanistic" educator.

Role of the Community-Junior College

To insure the quality and implementation of programs, universities must work closely with area community-junior colleges.

Community-junior colleges are usually quite willing to provide practicum and internship experiences for graduate students if these experiences are part of a well-designed university program and coordinated by knowledgeable and committed university personnel. Some community-junior colleges have even provided pay and staff supervision for graduate interns.

In addition to graduate internships, community-junior colleges can provide experienced staff members as resources for university classes. Projects and research studies can be carried out by graduate students in the community-junior college. Field trips, demonstrations, workshops, and interviews can all be provided by the community-junior college. Community-junior college facilities, laboratories, and materials are often more sophisticated than those available in the university.

The university must also develop cooperative relationships with business and industry, possibly through the community-junior college, for appropriate graduate programs. For those universities that have the programs and staff to prepare vocational and technical instructors, administrators, and counselors for the community-junior college, cooperation with business and industry is most important.

The community-junior college has another very important role in preservice programs. At many community-junior colleges, prospective instructors and paraprofessionals are currently students enrolled in the community-junior college. Therefore, programs which begin teacher education in these colleges need to be carefully coordinated with university programs to avoid duplication of efforts and to insure ease of student transfer. Universities and community-junior colleges should develop flexible but consistent career ladders to assist students as they explore the roles of paraprofessionals, instructors, or administrators.

A Teaching Degree for the Community-Junior College

Existing major degrees have not been appropriate for those who would *teach* in a community-junior college. The master's degree in a subject matter field often means too narrow course specialization and no instruction in the community-junior college and teaching methodology. Most subject matter degrees are lockstep routes for potential doctoral students in a discipline. On the other hand, the master of education degree has been criticized because it fails to offer sufficient preparation in the subject matter field.

The Ph.D. degree emphasizes specialized knowledge and research. Thus, it has been one of the least appropriate degrees for the community-junior college instructor. The Ph.D. has been the admission ticket into the professional ranks of the university; those whose goal is the "community of scholars" in the university experience "transfer shock" when they come to the community-junior college. The Ed.D. degree, while appropriate for administrators and counselors, suffers from the same limitation as the M.Ed.; it lacks sufficient depth in subject matter to make it an appropriate degree for instructors.

Degrees beyond the master's but less than the doctorate — Advanced Certificate, Specialist in Education, and the self-awarded A.B.D. — have been available for many years. They are not, however, degrees that have been held in high regard.

In recent years, new interest has developed in an advanced teaching degree that extends beyond the one-year master's and requires a different orientation than the research-based Ph.D. It is possible to redesign the Ph.D. as a teaching degree, but most effort has been in the direction of new degrees. Some colleges and universities have developed the two-year Master of Arts in College Teaching. Others have experimented with the Doctorate of Arts in Teaching. The Carnegie Corporation has provided considerable support for the development of D.A.T. programs in a number of universities. The D.A.T. degree is more likely to emerge as the favored degree of those who would teach in a community-junior college.

An advanced teaching degree appears to be ideally designed for the highly competent instructors required in the community-junior college. It is imperative, of course, that such degrees include the core of special experiences outlined in the preceding section. In addition, careful consideration should be given to the nature of the subject matter-content in these new degrees.

There is unanimous agreement that instructors coming to the community-junior college must be highly competent in their subject matter field. No one suggests that instructors should not be well grounded in knowledge of content. But too few question the validity of the kind of content in which these instructors are to be competent. An English instructor with thirty to forty hours of specialized graduate literature courses is not necessarily prepared to teach three sections of composition and one section of American literature in the community-junior college. How does a specialization in Medieval History help an instructor teach western civilization or American institutions or social problems? How does an advanced degree in experimental psychology help an instructor teach courses in personal development? Is the content of a degree in art history sufficient for the instructor of a course in humanities? Can a physics major bring the appropriate teaching competencies to a course in general science?

The problem extends beyond the failure of universities to supplement "content" courses with courses in the community-junior college and learning theory; most often, the "content" courses themselves are inappropriate for the needs of community-junior college faculty. Graduate students and community-junior college instructors need to question the traditional content of degree programs for the disciplines. They must work with willing colleges and universities to design more flexible and appropriate content programs for community-junior college instructors. It is to be hoped that the advanced teaching degree will be more than Ph.D. courses minus the dissertation; better, a new degree with different content and with a different purpose. Universities are not going to abandon the Ph.D., but with considerable financial support, many universities could develop a teaching Ph.D. or D.A.T. degree that could become a model preservice program for community-junior college instructors.

Cooperating Universities

If universities are to be chiefly responsible for the creation of quality preparation programs for community-junior college staff, then the universities must be qualified to do it. The following guidelines propose minimal qualifications for universities:

(1) *The university staff must be knowledgeable and experienced regarding the community-junior college.*

One of the great complaints regarding present university programs is that the professors coordinating these programs have no experience in the community-junior college. Scruggs [1969] surveyed 102 four-year colleges and universities that offered one or more courses in the community-junior college. Of 131 professors teaching these courses, only 7 had community-junior college experience; 81 had never been inside a community-junior college.

If universities wish to develop these programs, they should recruit qualified professionals from the community-junior colleges. This is no easy task because practitioners in the community-junior college often do not have the publishing and research backgrounds required for major positions in the universities. Too, universities can seldom offer salaries to match those earned by staff who hold leadership positions in community-junior colleges. Special funds must be available to the university so that these community-junior college leaders can be attracted to develop staff preservice programs.

If highly respected and knowledgeable community-junior college professionals cannot be attracted to the university, then these programs will encounter great difficulty in meeting the needs of the community-junior college.

(2) *The university must be willing to develop cooperative relationships with community-junior colleges.*

While universities have primary responsibility for program development, community-junior colleges have an important role to play in the preservice education of staff for these institutions. Key personnel from area community-junior colleges should be involved in all levels of University program planning. An advisory committee from these community-junior colleges should meet periodically with university staff to plan program objectives, determine curriculum, recruit staff and students, arrange facilities, provide internships, organize research, develop inservice programs which complement the preservice program, and develop evaluation schema for the preservice program.

Community-junior colleges should have primary responsibility for coordinating and supervising the university student internships. Funds should be available for supervision and for the interns' salaries to insure that the internship is a quality experience. The university should appoint key personnel in the community-junior college as adjunct university staff to encourage cooperation. Staff in many of the community-junior colleges have attained a high level of professionalization in the last decade and can be expected to perform supervisory roles as well as if not better than university staff.

(3) *The university should be adjacent to a number of outstanding community-junior colleges so that cooperative programs can be developed.*

If there is to be constant interaction between the university and the community-junior college, then it is more likely to occur when well-developed community-junior colleges are in close proximity to the university. Some of the best universities in the country have three or four community-junior colleges within commuting distance; some, especially in urban centers, have many more.

It is possible, of course, to provide internships in community-junior colleges which are not adjacent to the university, but close proximity is an advantage for the internship and for the many other cooperative relationships that should be developed.

(4) *The university should be an outstanding university in American education, or it should have some special attributes for developing a
program for community-junior college staff, or both.*

If a new degree for a new kind of person in a new kind of institution is to have any success, then it must have support from the
eminent universities in this country. The venture into the D.A.T.
cannot be left to the state colleges-lately-become-universities. Only
the major universities have, for the most part, the expertise in subject matter and in educational methodology which are needed in
these new staff development programs.

In the present decade, the great glut of Ph.D.s will force universities to re-examine their compulsive commitment to a one-dimen-
sional model of excellence. With available funds these universities
can be encouraged to develop the imaginative and nontraditional
preservice programs required for community-junior college staff.

There are some institutions of higher education that should be
encouraged to develop programs because of their special qualifications to do so. Examples include the Union Graduate School, upper-
level universities, and the California state colleges.

The Union Graduate School, based at Antioch College, is a
bold experiment in graduate education that offers a great deal of
promise for those who wish to be prepared for the community-
junior college. The School's program is creative and flexible. It provides a structure of education for graduate students which is similar
to the structure in which they will teach. The program experiences
are often based in community-junior colleges.

Upper-level universities have been designed to complement
community-junior colleges. Florida Atlantic University, the University of West Florida, Sangamon State University and Governor's
State University in Illinois, the new systems in Texas and Alaska
are examples, and others are being developed. These universities
are potential homes for significant community-junior college staff
development programs. They are dependent on the community-junior colleges, since they enroll no freshman or sophomore students.
They have developed excellent systems of cooperation with area
community-junior colleges. Their staffs often include personnel who
are knowledgeable and experienced in the community-junior college. These universities have not had time to become encrusted with
traditional graduate approaches to education. Finally, the great
majority of their students have attended community-junior colleges
and thus have at least some familiarity with the institution for which
their graduate program would be designed.

The California state colleges have a history of commitment to and involvement with the community-junior college movement. They have developed teacher education and student personnel programs that need to be continued and developed further.

A number of eminent and special colleges and universities meet the requirements outlined in this section. Many of them have been providing excellent staff preparation programs for a number of years. These programs should be expanded. However, if real impact is to be felt, a great many more programs will need to be developed in this decade.

Special Programs

A number of model graduate programs prepare community-junior college instructors, administrators, and student personnel workers. The great majority of programs should be designed for personnel in these general areas. There will be, however, a need for some programs which prepare educational specialists in the community-junior college. While a few community-junior college leaders feel that programs for specialists tend to foster a splintering effect among faculty, most leaders have recommended the preparation of specialists. Many specialists can be prepared through inservice programs and on-the-job experiences, but the need is sufficiently great to warrant immediate preservice programs in the areas outlined below:

(1) *Multi-Ethnic Program Coordinators*

Hundreds of community-junior colleges now offer special programs for black students and other minority groups. Hundreds more will develop programs in this decade as increasing numbers of minority students attend the community-junior college. Such programs require highly competent staff as coordinators.

Multi-ethnic programs are new to educational institutions. They need to be related to the ongoing program of the community-junior college. They must gain support from the institution and from the community. These programs are developed for a clientele that is often suspicious of administrators and instructors. Individual and social needs sometimes combine to challenge the most patient, supportive, and understanding of leaders in this field. To be even moderately successful, these programs require the most competent leaders available. Special preservice programs would make it possible to recruit promising candidates and prepare them for the task.

(2) *Remedial and Developmental Staff*

Most students who enter the two-year institution have "special needs" and are typically assigned to one or more remedial courses.

It is estimated that approximately 70–75 percent of all students in two-year institutions may be categorized as having "special needs."

From 40–60 percent of all students who enroll in remedial or preparatory English classes eventually receive a grade of D or F. Only 20 percent later enroll in credit English classes. Of these students, 75 percent withdraw the first year.

Sixty to seventy percent of all enrollees in two-year colleges do not complete the two-year program, and nine out of ten disadvantaged students are dropouts. [Carnell, 1969.]

These data hardly confirm the image of the community-junior college as the "people's college." The organization of successful programs of remedial and developmental education constitutes the most difficult challenge in educational programming to be faced by community-junior colleges in the decade of the seventies. Past success in these programs has been almost nonexistent. The purpose, the curriculum, and the learning strategies of these programs probably need complete redevelopment. This task is not likely to be accomplished until a sufficient number of very adequate staff are prepared in this area.

(3) *Staff Development Officers*

Although deans and division chairmen should assume responsibility for the continuing development of staff, their lack of training and their devotion to other duties keep them from doing so except in the most potent of community-junior colleges. As the need for staff development has become more and more recognized as a central concern of the institution, community-junior colleges have attempted to develop programs of inservice education on a continuing basis for staff. In some institutions a staff development officer has been appointed to coordinate these programs.

The primary purpose of the staff development officer is to develop and coordinate self-development programs for staff that lead to improved learning for students. Staff members want to improve their teaching, their administering, and their interpersonal relationships. They want to learn about new approaches to learning and new resources for assisting learning. Staff members want to make the institution all that it can be. If suitable guidance and appropriate recognition are provided, staff members will embrace a well designed and nonthreatening staff development plan with enthusiasm.

If staff development is to be more than a one-day preschool orientation session followed by an outside speaker several times a year, then staff development professionals need to be employed.

These staff may come from within the present community-junior college staff or elsewhere. Regardless of their prior employment, these development staff need special graduate preparation for their duties.

(4) *Human Development Specialists*

Many would argue that "human development" is everyone's job in an educational institution. Others would argue that when something is everyone's job then it is no one's job in particular and, therefore, it seldom gets done. In any case, in recent years, educational institutions have responded more and more to student requests for "meaningful and relevant" education by focusing on approaches to "affective" education. In some cases this response has resulted in institutionwide involvement in encounter groups. Some colleges have offered courses in human values; some have developed community service projects. Hundreds of community-junior colleges have turned old personal adjustment courses into new credit courses in self-development.

The human development specialist is an emerging model of the student personnel worker. He moves out of the counseling office to interact more openly with students and staff. He is responsible for teaching courses in the personal development curriculum which he has designed. He reviews institutional philosophy and structure and attempts to change overly restrictive or punitive rules, regulations, and grading practices. He helps students and staff to become involved in the community. He assists faculty members in becoming better instructors, providing feedback via televised class sessions, facilitating small groups, encouraging new material and new life styles.

In these ways, the human development specialist functions as a staff development officer. The two roles overlap because the purposes and approaches of each are similar. In small colleges one person could possibly serve both roles; in larger colleges a number of staff would be required for each role if the staff development or human development programs are to have any impact in the college.

(5) *Multimedia Specialists*

Many community-junior colleges currently house media resources which are overwhelming to the instructor who is still unsure of how to operate a tape recorder. In the 1970s, new media resources may project educational techniques beyond today's most imaginative expectations. If instructors are to have even a modicum of success in adapting these new media to their teaching, they will need assistance from specialists.

Multimedia specialists will not only have to know what media are available and how they operate; they will have to know how media can assist the instructor in improving the learning situation. They will have to be knowledgeable of curriculum, instructional strategies, and interpersonal relationships as they work with instructors who fear a "McLuhanesque nightmare."

(6) *Instructional Technology Specialists*

The Sputnik era helped to create a faith in technology as one cure of national education and social problems. During the 1960s, this faith was manifested in a new bloom of technological-educational innovations. Colleges experimented with the systems approach to learning, computer assisted instruction, audio-tutorial systems, management by objectives, and countless other structured experiences designed to increase learning in students. Often, these approaches helped to make the process of instruction more observable and, therefore, more open to change and improvement. Sometimes, the new instructional technologies helped to make certain kinds of learning more efficient and more effective.

The use of instructional technology will increase manyfold in the 1970s. If instructors are to take full advantage of this technology, they must be instructed in its use. Specialists will be required to stay abreast of new developments and to educate staff in the use of new approaches in instructional technology.

(7) *Health Occupations Staff*

While well-prepared staff will be needed at most levels of vocational-technical education, a primary need will be in the area of health occupations. Adequate health care has become one of the major goals of American society. To provide adequate health care in the nation, physicians must be assisted by a growing number of professional and paraprofessional staff. The great majority of the paraprofessionals will receive their education in community-junior colleges.

At the present time, the health occupation programs in community-junior colleges are coordinated and staffed by personnel who have been prepared as professional specialists: nurses, physical therapists, dentists, psychologists, etc. Because of their own preparation, these specialists are often not prepared to cope with a broadly defined program in health occupations. A preservice program is needed to introduce health occupations staff to the wide range of health occupations, to help them become competent in the core areas common to these various occupations, and to teach them to develop programs in the context of the community-junior college.

(8) *Community Outreach Program Coordinators*

The community-junior college has made a commitment to the inner city. It attempts to respond to the various needs of suburban centers. It often is the central focus for community activity in rural areas. If the word *"community"* in community-junior college is to have any relevance, then community outreach programs must multiply in great numbers in this decade. In his introduction of the Comprehensive Community College Act of 1969, Senator Harrison Williams [1969] of New Jersey said, "These institutions have demonstrated their potential to respond to society's changing needs in ways that bring improvement to the community."

The community-junior college can provide a forum for the community to examine its problems and act as a catalyst for the community to experiment with solutions. But before the community-junior college can assume such a challenging role, it must have staff who can create and implement community outreach programs. Michigan State University may be the only university in the nation that offers a program to prepare such staff. A number of additional programs are needed if community-junior colleges are to achieve their potential for community service.

(9) *Coordinators of Veterans' Services*

Through the AAJC Program for Servicemen and Veterans, Mallan [1971] reports that over one million service personnel a year are returning to civilian life from the armed services. A large proportion are from minority and educationally disadvantaged backgrounds. Most could not obtain educational deferments. Those having the least adequate educational background were frequently assigned responsibilities with little civilian job applicability. Unemployment among Vietnam-era veterans is more than twice the national average. The war is unpopular; their reception on college campuses is seldom warm, occasionally hostile. Three or four years absence from formal education frequently reduces their academic confidence. Upon discharge, about 40 percent either lack a high school education or have serious academic deficiencies. Minority veterans face even more acute problems in all three areas.

Mallan further reports that approximately 400,000 veterans are now enrolled in community-junior colleges. On many community-junior college campuses, between 25 and 50 percent of the full-time male student body are veterans. Many more could benefit from further education and training.

In order to provide adequate educational programs and service for these veterans, a professional staff member should be prepared to coordinate special services. Functions of a coordinator of veterans service would include recruitment, counseling, program planning, guidance in applying for veterans' benefits, establishment of special academic programs to which veterans are entitled, and assistance in establishing a life style commensurate with an educational institution.

With very few exceptions, there are no programs to prepare coordinators to assist returning veterans. With programs being established at military bases and on community-junior college campuses, the need for staff is considerable.

The list of specialists required for the community-junior college could be extended to include a variety of other areas. The specialists noted above seem to be in greatest demand at the moment. These specialists were mentioned most frequently by the thirty national community-junior colleges who responded to a memorandum requesting information for this report.

Other specialist areas suggested include state, regional and federal agency specialists; collective bargaining agents; institutional research officers; learning center administrators; budget, cost accounting, and management specialists; coordinators of cooperative education programs and adjunct staff; and a few others.

Many specialists are needed for the community-junior college, and special programs can help to prepare these specialists. But a note of caution from James Wattenbarger, Director of the Institute of Higher Education, University of Florida, should be taken into consideration:

Grants which are made tend to ride "hobby horses" which are currently popular. Emphasis on "developmental" education, "minority group" education, and other specialized areas sometimes tends to overshadow areas which are more universally needed. Programs should emphasize the total.

If these programs for specialists are developed within the context of a total program that includes the previously outlined dimensions for community-junior college staff, then there will be less chance for staff fragmentation and over-specialization. Indeed, the common core of program dimensions is as necessary, if not more so, for the specialists as it is for administrators, counselors, and instructors.

Paraprofessionals for the Community-Junior College

The community-junior college has made great progress in the past decade as one of the major centers for the preparation of technicians and professional aides in the nation. In the last few years, community-junior colleges have organized programs to prepare paraprofessionals for education — primarily as teacher aides for elementary and secondary schools. Now community-junior colleges are examining ways in which they can perpare paraprofessional staff for their own institutions.

As the education profession advances, special roles and tasks to facilitate learning become clearer. Master teachers become managers of learning. They supervise aides who arrange for equipment, lead small groups, evaluate and provide feedback on student performance, keep records, and provide individual tutoring. Administrators devote more time to long-range planning, staff relationships, goals and philosophy, community relationships, and program development, while assistants perform more shortrange tasks. Human development specialists facilitate groups of highly selected and experienced paraprofessional group facilitators who, in turn, facilitate several student groups each. The use of paraprofessionals to support professional staff and improve program effectiveness is a promising but relatively unexplored direction for staff development in the community-junior college.

Community-junior colleges should be encouraged to explore the use of paraprofessionals in their institutions. Those colleges that are qualified should be encouraged to prepare paraprofessionals. Paraprofessionals are already being educated and employed as counselor aides, teacher aides, media technicians, child-care center aides and learning center aides in some community-junior colleges. Models of these college preparation programs should be studied and tested in selected community-junior colleges. Model programs for the development of other paraprofessional groups should also be explored and tested.

The university and community-junior college should coordinate paraprofessional program requirements with the requirements of university programs. Many students will want to continue their education after their initial preparation as paraprofessionals. They should be able to do so with a minimum of difficulty. Paraprofessional programs should not be terminal programs. These programs offer an excellent opportunity for the early recruitment of students to a career in the community-junior college. The students will gain valuable experience as paraprofessionals; this experience can contribute immensely to the further development of full professionals for the community-junior college.

"Retooling" Ph.Ds. and New Staff from Business and Industry

Lewis Mayhew [1971] estimates that within a decade, the nation's colleges and universities will be producing 67,000 doctorates per year as compared to a 1968–69 total of 26,100. Moreover, he predicts that the present oversupply of Ph.D.'s in some fields could spread to all disciplines. This great abundance of doctorates has worried community-junior college leaders. Lyman Glenny [1971] states this concern:

As we look toward the next decade, it would be tragic, if not disastrous, for the surplus products of our research-oriented graduate schools to end up teaching in the junior and community colleges.

Committed to research, grounded in a discipline, educated in an elitist environment, and initiated into university academe, the Ph.D. is often the antithesis of the model staff member needed for the community-junior college. But it is sheer folly to assume that all Ph.D.'s are incapable of two-year college teaching. The Ph.D. is a highly motivated, intellectually gifted individual. He is, potentially, a competent staff member for the community-junior college. To be sure, his graduate preparation and, perhaps, some of his personal characteristics do not assist his development as a community-junior college staff member. But the Ph.D.-earner does not personify an immutable academic devil — even though he is caricatured as such by some community-junior college administrators, many of whom hold Ph.D.'s.

The present surplus of Ph.D.'s provides a pool of candidates from which the community-junior college can select many new staff members. Highly sophisticated selection procedures and well developed inservice programs can provide opportunities for Ph.D.'s to become competent staff members in the community-junior college. It also seems feasible to assume that preservice programs could be offered for the re-education of doctorates for community-junior college positions. Unable to find jobs which tap their abilities, Ph.D. degree holders should welcome a funded year of additional study that leads to challenging, rewarding work in the two-year college.

A number of year-long institutes should be funded to "retool" jobless Ph.D.'s for the community-junior college. The key to success for such a program is the selection of candidates. Careful screening techniques are absolutely essential to insure the selection of candidates whose philosophy, attitudes, values, and beliefs are consistent with those of the community-junior college. A panel of master teachers and administrators from community-junior colleges could provide invaluable assistance in the selection process.

After promising candidates were selected, the re-education program could be organized to include an understanding and acceptance of the community-junior college and its students, an internship in the community-junior college, an understanding of the learning process and of new approaches and innovations in education, and experiences in the facilitation of human development. Thus, in one year, these candidates could return to the job market with skills that are employable and the motivation that is essential to the fulfillment of the social promise of the community-junior college.

Many staff members come from business and industry to work in the community-junior college. These staff share some characteristics with the Ph.D. earners. They, too, are highly specialized in some area, usually an area in the vocational-technical program. They share the Ph.D.s' lack of understanding of the community-junior college and its students. They, too, are inexperienced in teaching and learning processes. They have probably developed life styles which are marked by the competitive spirit of the economic marketplace; many Ph.D.'s have also developed life styles which reflect the competitiveness of the academic marketplace and graduate school.

Of course, there are important differences between the two groups — practical vs. theoretical, liberal arts vs. vocational, B.A. vs. Ph.D. — but there are enough similarities to warrant experimentation with a program designed to include representatives of both groups. The interaction between these two groups may be particularly creative and educational as it affords an experiential laboratory for synthesizing and integrating the comprehensive nature of the community-junior college. On the other hand, if a combined program does not seem feasible, then consideration should be given to organizing experimental programs for each of these groups. A highly competent and deeply committed staff could be the considerable payoff of such experimentation.

Inservice Programs

In the decade of the 1970s, the preservice programs for community-junior college staff will need to be greatly expanded. Present programs need to be developed in a variety of areas, primarily for instructors. It is the contention of the authors of this report, however, that *programs for the 70's should focus on inservice education*. Community-junior colleges employed approximately 130,000 staff members in the fall of 1971. Although most of these staff members had completed their preservice educational experiences, all of them needed continuing inservice educational experiences.

All staff members, the mediocre and the highly competent, need continuing opportunities to keep up with new developments in education. Community-junior colleges tend to be innovative; they tend to be willing to explore nontraditional approaches to learning. With increasing new developments in curriculum, instructional technology, organizational patterns, facilities and equipment, and teaching-learning styles, (many of which have been developed by and for community-junior colleges), it is imperative that staff have opportunities to learn about and to adapt these innovations to their situation.

As pointed out in earlier sections of this report, vast numbers of community-junior college staff members are performing at mediocre and, in too many cases, inadequate levels. These people need basic inservice programs to upgrade and retool their skills, attitudes, and knowledge.

The key people in the community-junior college are the highly competent and creative staff members who provide leadership, encourage community, and develop quality programs at the college. Special effort should be made to design appealing inservice programs that utilize and enhance their competency. Master teachers need renewal and reward or they will grow dull and cynical; what is worse, they may become clock punchers rather than exemplars for other staff members.

Priority needs to be given to inservice programs also because preservice programs will not graduate enough staff to meet the needs of community-junior colleges for this decade and probably not the next. Too, many preservice programs will not prepare staff appropriately for community-junior college employment. These staff will need inservice education to develop the necessary skills, attitudes, and understandings which are required by the community-junior college.

Finally, inservice education should be strongly supported because it provides the best opportunity for community-junior colleges to renew and expand their programs. "Improved personal development leads to improved program development." [O'Banion, 1971.] Unless staff members are constantly updated and supported in their own development, programs cannot grow and flourish to meet the needs of students. The administration that places more value on staff than on buildings, organizational plans, increased enrollments, instructional technology, and public image increases the chance for the institution to have a significant impact on students.

If inservice programs are to be designed to meet the needs noted above, primary responsibility must be assumed by the community-junior college. Staff development must be important enough for the college to integrate it as a primary activity; otherwise, it remains outside the college, a service of the university. The community-junior college must define its own needs for staff development, and must provide the basic funds to support programs. The university, state departments, and other agencies can provide assistance, but the best inservice programs are likely to be indigenous operations.

An Inservice Program in Every College

A dean from an eastern community-junior college said recently:

In 1969 and 1970 we had a semiorganized program for new faculty to acquaint them with the junior college, rules and regulations, types of students, types of problems, etc. This year with so few new faculty we did not hold any meetings but depended upon the department chairmen to provide any inservice opportunities.

This description is not atypical of inservice programs in community-junior colleges across the nation. Some colleges provide no inservice opportunities; most provide at least an orientation program preceding the beginning of fall classes; some even provide for periodic programs during the year and allow staff members to attend off-campus programs; too few provide a well-designed, strongly supported, total institution inservice program.

Poor programs abound for many reasons. One primary reason is the lack of leadership among top administrators. Many presidents assume an avuncular role and see inservice education as a one-day orientation session where they welcome new staff to join "the little family" of distinguished faculty. Or programs are organized by the academic dean and department heads to relay information. A consultant from a nearby university or neighboring community-junior college may be invited to speak about the mission of the community-junior college or the nature of the community-junior college student, and inservice education is not considered again until next year.

Administrators support poor programs also by helping to perpetuate blind salary schedules which reward only the quantity, not the quality of accumulated graduate course hours. Staff members take all kinds of university evening and extension courses because fifteen more credit hours mean so many more dollars on the salary scale. The resulting hodgepodge of university courses should not be rewarded more than coordinated inservice experiences. But, university courses that fit into a well designed, individually tailored, employer-college supervised, continuing education program are, on the other had, most appropriate for staff and salary advancement.

If staff development is to be effective, then someone must assume major responsibility for coordinating the program. An assistant to the president, the academic dean, a special committee from the faculty council, or a staff development officer should be clearly in charge. The program should be a continuing program throughout the year and should be related to long-range improvement in the college. The program should be designed to achieve institutional goals through the development of individual staff members. Many group activities may be available, but each staff member should have a program for his personal inservice development. Rupert Evans [1970] says, "It should be the responsibility of every administrator to build, in cooperation with each staff member, an individualized staff development plan covering at least five years."

The purpose of the staff development program is, ultimately, to enhance the opportunities for student development at the college through the professional development of each college staff member. This purpose is best achieved, as Alice Thurston, President of Garland College in Boston, has said, "in a total institutional climate which is characterized by trust, respect, and a deep concern for people." When the climate of learning for the staff is open, flexible, affirming, challenging; the climate of learning for students is likely to be similar.

Staff development programs should be integrated with evaluation processes to allow the individual and the college to determine progress. Such programs must not be "seek and destroy" missions but should focus on development. Arthur Cohen [1971], Director of the Junior College ERIC at University of California at Los Angeles, has said, "I don't see instructor evaluation or training as some kind of reward-punishment cycle. It's all reward. It has to be. You're not setting up evaluation schemes or training schemes in order to gather evidence on which to punish people or fire people."

The aim is to develop a program that is so integrated into the fabric of the college that staff accept as normal the opportunity to plan goals and carry out activities that help them improve their teaching, administering and counseling. When the rewards are clear, and opportunities are provided, staff members will choose to be innovative and creative. When staff members begin to grow and develop, the college will move toward increased potency and impact.

An efficient and effective program of staff development requires, of course, considerable funds. In the past, staff development programs have been classed as low priority programs and thus, have received few funds. In the past, staff development programs have been classed as low priority programs and thus, have received few funds. In general, this low priority status has been maintained during the present high competition for budget dollars. An important exception, however, has occurred in Florida. There, the state legislature has allocated special funds for staff development programs in all Florida community-junior colleges.

Florida's example must be followed: funds must be available to state departments of education, universities, and community-junior colleges if staff development programs are to become a reality in this decade. Some states may be able to follow Florida's lead, but most states will need assistance from the federal government if they are to help the community-junior colleges to develop inservice development programs which have a useful impact upon the staff and the college.

State Support for Inservice Education

Every state in the nation has a community-junior college, and every college in every state should have an inservice program for staff development. The states can help the individual colleges through the development of comprehensive, statewide plans for staff inservice education. These plans should be developed by the units responsible for community-junior colleges in state departments of education. The units should develop plans which coordinate the efforts of state colleges and universities, staff professional associations, other state agencies, regional laboratories and agencies, and individual community-junior colleges. For example, state universities often duplicate inservice efforts; this duplication could be avoided in a coordinated state plan.

The Comprehensive Community College Act of 1969 placed high priority on a state plan for staff development. The Act called for a master plan for community-junior college development in each state.

The master plans will be developed jointly at the State level with all postsecondary education agencies within that State. They will set forth a statewide plan for the improvement, development, and construction of comprehensive community colleges, including first, the development and implementation of comprehensive curriculum programs that have a special emphasis on the needs of the educationally and economically disadvantaged; second, the training and development of faculty and staff; . . . [Williams, 1969.]

The Florida plan for staff development could serve as a model for other states. During the 1968 Special Session of the Florida Legislature, Senate Bill 76X(68) was enacted which provided funds for Staff and Program Development. The Board of Education stated that the "purpose of this program is to improve the total effectiveness of the college curriculum through the continuing development and improvement of faculty, staff and program." Thus the relationship between program improvement and staff improvement was clearly recognized by the Florida Board.

A statewide committee developed and implemented guidelines for the use of Florida funds in the 1969–70 academic year. Each college in the state is required to formulate a long-range plan for development including a statement of the college philosophy and objectives. The college must indicate its goal priorities for staff and program development. Specific projects and activities for achieving the goals must be described in detail. Finally, the college is required to determine its procedures for evaluating goals achievement or for choosing alternatives along with a budget. The final, total plan for development is submitted to the Florida Division of Community Colleges for review and approval.

One college has implemented this new program in a way which is exemplary of the level of sophistication which individual colleges can achieve when funds are available to stimulate their growth and development. At Santa Fe Junior College in Gainesville, Florida, a nine-member Task Force for Staff and Program Development coordinates the inservice program with a chairman who has primary responsibility for staff development.

All staff members in the college participated in developing the long-range goals and the philosophy and objectives of the institution. Staff members are encouraged to submit proposals for goal-related program and staff development projects to the Task Force. The Task Force uses the following criteria to determine which staff projects will be funded:

(1) evidence that plans or projects primarily affect the total college,

(2) identifiable needs in the present program,

(3) evidence that all areas of the college — certificated, noncertificated, and administrative — were represented, and

(4) evidence that evaluative procedures were considered. [Santa Fe Junior College, 1969.]

In 1970–71, the Task Force funded twenty special projects at Santa Fe — including new staff orientation, team visitation, environmental studies, nonacademic inservice training programs, workshops and institutes, faculty inservice, community relations, League faculty exchange program, programs for paraprofessionals in social agencies, student affairs, psychiatric consultant, multidisciplinary, teaching-learning center, development of parent-child training centers, interinstitutional research activities, and others relating to curriculum or materials development.

These projects, supported and coordinated by the college, provide creative opportunities for staff to explore and experiment with new approaches to learning and teaching. Such opportunities should be available for all community-junior colleges. The staff and program development plan in the State of Florida provides a model to be duplicated and improved upon in other states.

Types of Inservice Programs

Inservice education programs have multiplied rapidly in recent years. There is a great potpourri of one-day seminars, three-day conventions, and week-long workshops which attempt to meet inservice needs. Almost any program offered has a ready audience. Tens of thousands of educators attend hundreds of conventions and workshops each year. Educational entrepreneurs have even formed "educational corporations" which offer "relevant" workshops. Although fees are often exorbitant, attendance is high.

If this great diversity of offerings is to be more useful to the community-junior college, there should be some long-range planning to insure the wise selection and use of programs. At the present time universities and agencies offer programs more on the basis of current issues or what is available than on what the staff really needs. Community-junior college staff are invited to participate in these programs and they usually do. But more attention should be given to the specific needs of community-junior college staff, before programs are planned.

Inservice needs should be determined for each college. To determine institutional needs each staff member should produce a self-development plan in consultation with those responsible for staff and program development in the college. The staff member's personal program of development is the basis of the college program which, in turn, is the basis of the statewide plan for development. The state plan is managed by the department of education which provides leadership in the distribution of funds and coordination of state services. Comprehensive, coordinated state planning is necessary or programs will continue to be offered on a piece-meal basis, providing little satisfaction for the colleges and staffs who wish to upgrade, renew, and develop more fully.

In the following section, different types of inservice programs are described and recommendations offered for their development. The general recommendation of the section is that all of these programs will be more useful if they have been designed in response to clearly defined college needs which relate to well developed individual staff development plans.

(1) *Institutes, Summer and Year-Long*

Institutes provide an excellent opportunity for concentrated study and have proved to be one of the more popular inservice approaches under EPDA. Institutes are usually held in the summer (4, 6, or 8 weeks long) or in periodic sessions throughout the year. They usually focus on a special area and are held on the campus of a university or community-junior college. University credit is often available.

Institute participants often learn a great deal from each other because different colleges from different states are represented. But the transfer of learning back to individual college campuses may not be great. If an individual attends the institute and becomes enthused about an idea, he may find little support at his home college when he attempts to import the idea single-handedly. To provide for greater institute impact, campus teams should attend the institute for a specific purpose and work on a specific project. The team approach will more likely result in home college program change.

Summer institutes often offer little more than two regular graduate courses, a few consultants, and a field trip or two. For many educators the summer institute is a vacation and an opportunity to add six more credit hours to his salary scale. Summer institutes should be designed to meet the real needs of community-junior college staff. One of the functions of the state department might be to identify and summarize major needs, and then recommend institutes at colleges which can meet those needs. Institute experiences should probably provide a more intense experience for those attending. The models of "intensive education" developed by the Peace Corps, VISTA, the military, and business and industry should be adapted to the summer institute.

(2) *Short Term Workshops*

In contrast to institutes, workshops usually focus on a more specific topic and are usually of shorter duration. Workshops are most appropriate as means for introducing new ideas or for implementing new approaches and devices. They are very helpful in keeping staff up-to-date regarding innovations and new developments in community-junior college education.

(3) *Staff Retreats*

Staff retreats are particularly helpful in building staff harmony and enthusiasm at the college. Sometimes the staff from a department or special program will spend several days away from campus, often in isolation, to review objectives and philosophy and to explore new programs. Sometimes the total college staff and many students will be involved in a retreat.

At Flathead Valley Community College in Montana, the total staff lives on a dude ranch for several days prior to the opening of classes. The atmosphere is informal and there is a great deal of socializing for new staff. During the retreat, staff members meet in small groups to explore and determine the major college goals to be achieved during the coming year. These goals are agreed upon by the group, and clear responsibility for their implementation is designated. On the final day, board members join the staff. These retreat sessions provide invaluable opportunities which enhance communication among staff members, develop a sense of community and commitment, and encourage the assessment of the major goals of the college. In addition to other rewards of the retreat, these sessions provide an excellent orientation experience for new faculty.

(4) *Inhouse Continuing Seminars*

Some community-junior colleges offer on-campus continuing seminars or courses to help develop special staff understanding or skills. In some cases the university is called in to offer an extension course. At Miami-Dade Junior College in Florida, community-junior college staff members have been appointed by the University of Miami to teach specialized extension courses to community-junior college staff when university staff were not available. At De Anza College in California, staff members can enroll in special inservice courses that are designed to develop instructional materials and methods. Staff enrollees receive community-junior college credit for these courses — credit which counts on their salary scale. The approach at De Anza could serve as a model for other community-junior colleges that wish to develop serious inservice education programs.

(5) *Encounter Groups*

In the past five years, the encounter group or sensitivity training session has been widely used in education. The encounter group has been used to improve administrative relationships, improve teaching styles, encourage innovation and change, and explore special concerns such as black-white relationships and student-staff relationships. The encounter approach offers an excellent way to assist staff members in exploring the nature and impact of their attitudes, values, and beliefs upon their relationships with students and other staff. Some colleges, specifically dedicated to developing a humanistic institution with a humanistic staff, have relied heavily on the encounter group to facilitate change.

Approximately 75 percent of the staff at El Centro College in Dallas have participated in encounter groups. In one case twelve administrators spent three days in an encounter group led by two outside facilitators. Following this first laboratory, the twelve administrators — including the president — were divided into six pairs. Each pair then participated in another three-day laboratory with a professional facilitator and groups comprised mainly of faculty members at the College. Outside researchers later interviewed the faculty members and asked, "Have you observed any changes in the behavior of some of the administrators since the laboratories?" In nearly all cases, the faculty were able to cite specific indications of changed behavior. They also seemed to agree that the changes were positive and beneficial. The El Centro administrators were described as more honest, open, better able to listen, more capable of helping people get to the real problems with which they were concerned, and more efficient in facilitating cooperative decisions. [Hendrix and Stanley, 1969.]

At El Centro, the encounter group has become a major vehicle for improved staff relationships. The encounter group can also be used as an orientation device to involve new faculty in a more creative way with the College. Such groups encourage new faculty to share their concerns and become acquainted with each other as well as the continuing faculty.

(6) *Conventions and Professional Meetings*

While conventions and professional meetings are probably not as effective as longer term, more focused inservice programs, they are important aspects of any well designed inservice program. Conventions provide great stimulation in that in a very brief period of time staff are exposed to a wide variety of ideas, projects and people. Contacts are made, visitations are encouraged, materials are exchanged, ideas are debated and confirmed.

Moreover, there is an opportunity for the staff member to get away from the daily work on campus and gain perspective on goals and activities. The profession of education requires a constant response to a multitude of colleagues and students; there is seldom time for contemplation and long-range review. Conventions and professional meetings provide important opportunities for staff renewal.

(7) *Visitations*

Many community-junior colleges encourage their staff to visit other colleges to observe and review educational programs. Some community-junior colleges have become so well known for their special programs that they entertain visitors every week of the year. First hand opportunities to review programs in action are most effective in stimulating programs and staff development at many community-junior colleges.

Colleges need to be aware of and have access to model programs in community-junior colleges. Model programs in developmental education, audiotutorial systems, community outreach programs, student personnel programs, career programs, faculty evaluation, black studies, special facilities, and other areas need to be identified and examined. Professionals have an informal communication which identifies some of the major centers of innovation and creativity, but a formal system should be initiated to help those colleges in greatest need to identify the model centers. State departments of education may be able to help initiate this system. If model centers can be identified, then staff members in these centers should receive funds to develop inservice experiences for other colleges.

Model staff development programs should be especially identified for other colleges. Some colleges should be selected to develop programs which explain their model inservice programs to teams sent from interested colleges to review and adapt the inservice model to their colleges. One particularly stimulating approach would be to identify five or six model college programs and then provide a showcase tour for top administrators from colleges considering staff development programs.

(8) *Packaged Programs*

New developments in media, instructional technology, and behavioral objectives have important implications for organizing staff development programs. The T. V. College of the City Colleges of Chicago has developed a series of television tapes using major consultants to discuss the major functions of the community-junior college. Santa Fe Junior College in Florida has produced a nominally priced series of cassette recordings of national leaders discussing their perceptions of the most important problem facing the community-junior college in the 1970s. These packages should not substitute for inservice programs but they could complement a well designed program.

One very innovative package approach has been utilized in a pilot project at Delaware Technical Institute. Programmed learning units have been developed to acquaint new faculty with the community and the college. New faculty use these units any time and at their own rate. These programs show that new learning approaches for students may also be utilized for faculty learning. Other special programmed units could be developed on the history and philosophy of the community-junior college, the nature and characteristics of community-junior college students, and innovations in teaching. These programs would be of general use to a wide variety of institutions. Such units would be particularly helpful for new faculty in their "period of adjustment" to the community-junior college. Other units could be developed for special areas.

(9) *Apprenticeships*

A most effective inservice program for new staff can be developed around an apprenticeship system. Mature colleges that have developed good evaluation schemes and recognize and reward competency will have identified the master or lead instructors. In a well designed staff development program, these master instructors could serve as guides and tutors for new apprentice staff. But the master-apprentice teacher relationship must be more than an informal, off-the-cuff relationship, or the program is likely to deteriorate into an occasional conference, if, indeed, it ever develops to that extent. If the master-apprentice relationships are important enough to gain college support — recognition, released time, evaluation, encouragement — and be integrated into the permanent design of the college, then apprenticeship programs can serve two main purposes: they can provide recognition for highly competent staff, and quality inservice education for new staff.

(10) *Professional Reading*

A time-honored but often overlooked approach to inservice education is through professional reading. In the last ten years the amount and quality of literature on the community-junior college, and in education in general, has increased enormously. Many colleges purchase group subscriptions to the *Junior College Journal*. Other colleges provide a special professional library. A basic community-junior college professional library should be identified so that colleges can begin organizing these resources for staff. In a well designed, college-wide staff development program, the professional library will be a necessary and a central component.

Conclusion

These are the major inservice approaches to staff development. There are others, of course, and hopefully more and more creative approaches are being developed.

While it is important to note the types of programs offered, it is also important to note that these programs can best be used when certain prior conditions exist. As has been noted, inservice programs are too often offered by universities and other agencies without much consideration for the real staff and college needs which will be served. If inservice programs are to be fully effective, then they need much more development, integration, and organization than they receive at present. First, these programs must be given much higher priority than they have at present. Funds must be available to convert potshot inservice experiences into meaningful inservice education programs. Second, these programs must be integrated into the fiber of the college. The basis for this integration must be the individual staff member's specification of his personal needs and plans for long-range professional development. Third, inservice programs must be better organized — eventually at the state level. Every state department of education has a unit responsible for community-junior colleges. This unit should receive a block of federal funds to assist its identification of outstanding programs, allocation of funds for program development and coordination of all services for this development.

Commitment to inservice (and preservice) program development is vital at all levels: the individual, the college, the state — and the federal. Through the allocation of funds, the federal government can spur the development of preservice and inservice staff education programs. In so doing, it will spur the community junior college to move more quickly toward its realization as the "people's college."

References

Carnell, Paul H., Chairman, Junior and Community College Task Force. *Junior and Community College Report* Memorandum to Peter P. Muirhead, Acting Deputy Commissioner of Education, May 26, 1969.

Cohen, Arthur. "Recorded Interview with Gregory Goodwin," UCLA, November 19, 1971.

Evans, Rupert in *Seminar on Graduate Education Programs,* (ed.) Joseph P. Arnold, Leadership Training Series No. 30, Columbus, Ohio: Ohio State University, 1970.

Glenny, Lyman. "Doctoral Planning for the 1970's," *Research Reporter,* 6 (1971): 4.

Hendrix, Vernon L. and Stanley, William H. *Group Dynamics — Communications Laboratories for Administrators at El Centro College: A Report to the Hogg Foundation,* Dallas County Junior College District, August 4, 1969.

Mallan, John P. "Memorandum" AAJC Program for Servicemen and Veterans. November 11, 1971.

Mayhew, Lewis. "The Degree Glut — A Forecast," *Behavior Today,* November 16, 1971.

O'Banion, Terry. *New Directions in Community College Student Personnel Programs,* American College Personnel Association: Washington, D.C. Student Personnel Series No. 15, 1971.

Santa Fe Junior College. *Staff Development Plan 1969–70.* Office of Research and Development: Gainesville, Florida, July, 1969.

Scruggs, M. W. "A Survey of the Number of University Professors in Teacher Training Institutions Who Have Community College Experience." Forest Park Community College: St. Louis, 1969.

Williams, Harrison. "Introduction of Comprehensive Community College Act of 1969, S. 1033." *Congressional Record — Senate,* February 17, 1969, 3435.

7. Summary of Recommendations

This report outlines the need and indicates directions for the development of community-junior staff. The needs identified appear to be so crucial and so extensive that massive effort from many agencies will be required if the needs are to be met.

Needs

As has been indicated elsewhere in this report, the increase in numbers of students attending the community-junior college has been overwhelming. In 1970, approximately 2,500,000 students attended 1,091 community-junior colleges. Approximately 122,400 staff members provided educational services for these students.

While there are various estimates for increases in students, colleges, and staff by 1980, it is generally accepted that students and staff will double in size during the decade. By 1980, it has been estimated that 4,450,000 students will be attending 1,371 community-junior colleges. Staff required for these colleges will number 216,100. During the 1970s, therefore, 93,700 new staff members, of which 16,000 will be administrators and service personnel, will be required for the community-junior college. At least 9,370 new staff members will be needed each year for the next ten years.

It is clear from this report that programs to prepare these community-junior college staff personnel, 93,700 new staff by 1980 and 122,400 existing staff, are virtually non-existent. Kelly and Connolly (1970) estimate that present preservice programs place only about 150 new faculty a year in the community-junior college. In the EPDA 1971–72 Part E programs (institutes, shortterm training programs, and special projects) only two programs for 75 personnel were especially designed for the preservice education of community-junior college personnel.

The programs for inservice education reflect the greater need for inservice development, but the response from EPDA is less than satis-factory. In 1971–72, only 3,453 staff members participated in institutes, shortterm training programs and special projects designed specifically for the community-junior college under Part E of EPDA at a cost of $2,422,305. An additional 2,578 staff members participated in similar programs at a cost of $1,801,912, but these programs were designed for staff members from community-junior colleges *and* four-year colleges. Assuming that half these staff members were from community-junior colleges, only 4,742 community-junior college staff members were pro-vided inservice experience under EPDA in 1970–71. Therefore, *only 4 percent* of the existing 122,400 staff members benefited from the inser-vice education portion of EPDA. If only 25 percent of present staff were to be provided inservice experience under this portion of EPDA, appro-priations would have to be increased by $17,500,000. As stated in the first paragraph of this chapter, *"massive* effort from many agencies will be required if the needs are to be met."

The need for staff development is particularly acute if the com-munity-junior college is to implement this society's commitment to the academically deficient and the socioeconomically disadvantaged.

Approximately 70–75 percent of all students in two-year colleges are in need of remedial or compensatory programs. Sixty to 70 percent of all enrollees become dropouts. *Nine out of ten disadvantaged students become dropouts.* The reasons for the high attrition rate in two-year colleges are:

(1) Poorly trained instructors who are not interested in students as individuals and who believe that the disadvantaged cannot learn.

(2) Poorly designed courses that in most cases are completely inadequate for the special needs of the disadvantaged. [*The Junior/Community College Task Force,* 1969.]

Recommendations

In the previous chapter many recommendations for staff develop-ment programs are suggested. Other recommendations are implied in the discussion. In this section, priority recommendations are summarized.

Two major recommendations provide the framework for those that follow:

(1) While the development of new preservice programs for the prepara-tion of community-junior colleges is important in the 1970's, priority should be given to the development of a variety of creative and well-designed inservice programs.

(2) In both preservice and inservice programs, priority should be given to staff development which helps serve the special needs of socioeconomically and educationally disadvantaged students. Special attention should be given to the recruitment of minority staff members, not only for special programs, but for appointment in transfer, career, and counseling programs as well as in administrative positions.

Inservice Programs

(1) Every state should have a staff development program coordinated by the unit in the state department of education responsible for community-junior colleges. It should be the purpose of the state program to insure that every college has a staff development program. The program developed by the state of Florida could serve as a national model.

(2) Every staff member in every community-junior college should have a professional development plan, individually tailored in terms of the goals and resources of the college and the needs of the individual staff member. Such a plan should be developed in consultation with appropriate college officials and should form the basis for staff evaluation.

(3) The most creative and potent staff development programs in community-junior colleges should be identified to serve as models. Descriptions of these models should be disseminated, and opportunities for visitation should be provided.

(4) The most creative and potent programs in remedial and developmental education, staff evaluation, student personnel, media centers, use of behavioral objectives, instructional technology, and other pertinent areas should be identified, information about them disseminated, and opportunities for visitation provided.

(5) Highly competent consultants in all areas in which development is needed should be identified, and information regarding their experience and expertise should be made available.

(6) Programmed packages on the history and philosophy of the community-junior college, the nature and characteristics of community-junior college students, innovations in teaching, and a variety of other areas should be developed to complement inservice programs.

(7) The proposed Institute of Higher Education or other appropriate agencies should study the professional development needs of various community-junior college staff groups to identify the major needs of new career and mid-career staff.

(8) A study should be undertaken to determine the inservice opportunities available to community-junior college staff through the Area Manpower Institutes for Development of Staff; the regional educational laboratories; business, labor, and industry training centers; universities and community-junior colleges; and other agencies.

(9) A variety of institutes, workshops, retreats, and forums on a variety of topics should be offered to community-junior college staff throughout the year in major regions of the country. The Danforth summer institute and the Bennet Conference are models to be duplicated.

(10) If these recommendations are to be acted upon, a coordinating agency should assume responsibility for nationwide planning to insure development of these types of programs most in demand and most needed by community-junior college staff. A major university, the American Association of Junior Colleges, or a special community-junior college unit in the United States Office of Education could be the coordinating agency.

Preservice Programs

(1) Selected universities should be funded to develop model preservice programs for community-junior college staff. These programs should be designed specifically for community-junior colleges. The Junior College Leadership Programs for administrators should be continued and similar models developed for instructors, student personnel workers, and other education specialists.

(2) The advanced teaching degree should become the model degree for community-junior college instructors. Programs similar in goals to those of the D.A.T. should be developed in major universities and especially in the new upper division universities.

(3) A few universities should develop special programs for special staff to include Ethnic Program Coordinators, Remedial and Developmental Staff, Staff Development Officers, Human Development Specialists, Multimedia Specialists, Instructional Technology Specialists, Health Occupations Staff, Community Outreach Program

Coordinators, and Coordinators of Cooperative Education Programs.

(4) Qualified community-junior colleges should design and test programs to prepare paraprofessionals to work in the community-junior college. Programs are needed to prepare counselor and teacher aides, media technicians, learning center aides, and aides to staff college-based child care centers.

(5) Special year-long institutes should be developed in selected universities to re-educate selected surplus Ph.D.'s and new staff from business and industry for the community-junior college.

(6) The outstanding community-junior colleges which are staffed by master community-junior college instructors and administrators should be identified. These colleges should serve as internship sites for preservice programs.

References

Higher Education Personnel Training Programs 1971–1972. Institute, Short-Term Training Program, Special Projects, EPDA, U.S.O.E.

The Junior/Community College Task Force. A Joint Report of the United States Office of Education and the American Association of Junior Colleges, May 1969.

Appendix A. Highest Degree: Community-Junior College Faculty 1960–70

(in percentages)

Year and Author	Doctorate	Masters	Less Than Masters	Total
1961 (Siehr)	7	73	20	100
1963 (Wattenbarger)	12	77	11	100
1964 (Brown)	11	75	14	100
1965 (Kelly)	7	68	25	100
1966 (Beazley)	6	74	20	100
1966 (Anderson and Spencer — part-time only)	4	70	26	100
1966 (Anderson and Spencer — full-time only)	6	89	5	100
1967 (Anderson and Spencer — part-time only)	5	71	24	100
1967 (Anderson and Spencer — full-time only)	5	88	7	100
1967 (Beazley)	6	76	18	100
1967 (NSF)	9	74	17	100
1967 (Phair)	3	76	21	100
1968 (Phair)	4	78	18	100
1968 (Anderson and Thornblad)	4	77	19	100
1969 (Martin and Thornblad)	6	69	25	100
1969 (IBHE)	4	77	19	100
1969 (Phair)	5	75	20	100
1970 (Phair)	5	75	20	100
1970 (Medsker and Tillery)	9	78	13	100
1970 (IJCB)	6	66	28	100

Appendix B. Sources of Junior College Faculty

(in percentages)

Year and Author	Public School Systems	Comm. Colleges	Senior Inst.	Grad. School	Business, Industry and Other	Total
1961 (Siehr)	33	7	11	21	28	100
1964 (NSF)	33				67	100
1965 (NEA)	30		17	24	29	100
1968 (Farris)	15		46			inc.
1967 (Good)	86					inc.
1967 (Phair)	38	19	15	8	20	100
1968 (Phair)	36	19	19	8	18	100
1969 (Phair)	33	22	19	7	19	100
1970 (Phair)	26	30	18	8	18	100
1966 (Anderson and Spencer) Part-time	44	15	5	0	36	100
1966 Full-time	43	11	16	10	20	100
1967 Part-time	42	7	8	0	43	100
1967 Full-time	36	15	22	8	19	100
1969 (Martin and Thornblad)	34	13	19	9	25	100
1970 (IJBC)	23	13	18	11	35	100

Appendix C. Institutions Offering Graduate Degree Programs

The following colleges and universities have recently indicated to the Association their sponsorship of one or more graduate programs for the preparation of community-junior college instructors. There may be others on which no information is now available. Inclusion in this list implies neither approval nor disapproval of any program by the Association.

Antioch College
Yellow Springs, Ohio

Appalachian State University
Boone, North Carolina

Arizona State University
Tempe, Arizona

Auburn University
Auburn, Alabama

Boston College
Chestnut Hill, Massachusetts

Brigham Young University
Provo, Utah

Carnegie-Mellon University
Pittsburgh, Pennsylvania

College of William and Mary
Williamsburg, Virginia

Columbia University
(Teachers College)
New York, New York

Drake University
Des Moines, Iowa

Duke University
Durham, North Carolina

East Carolina University
Greenville, North Carolina

Eastern Illinois University
Charleston, Illinois

Eastern Washington State College
Cheney, Washington

Emory University
Atlanta, Georgia

Florida State University
Tallahassee, Florida

Illinois State Normal University
Normal, Illinois

Indiana University
Bloomington, Indiana

Kansas State Teachers College
Emporia, Kansas

Lehigh University
Bethlehem, Pennsylvania

Michigan State University
East Lansing, Michigan

Mississippi State University
State College, Mississippi

Northern Arizona University
Flagstaff, Arizona

Northern Illinois University
DeKalb, Illinois

Ohio State University
Columbus, Ohio

Oklahoma State University
Stillwater, Oklahoma

Oregon State University
Corvallis, Oregon

Pennsylvania State University
University Park, Pennsylvania

Purdue University
Lafayette, Indiana

Rhode Island College
Providence, Rhode Island

Rochester Institute of Technology
Rochester, New York

Rutgers — The State University
New Brunswick, New Jersey

Sacramento State College
Sacramento, California

Sam Houston State College
Huntsville, Texas

San Diego State College
San Diego, California

San Jose State College
San Jose, California

Sarah Lawrence College
Bronxville, New York

Southern Illinois University
Carbondale, Illinois

Stephen F. Austin State State College
Nacogdoches, Texas

University of Alabama
Birmingham, Alabama

University of Arizona
Tucson, Arizona

University of California
Berkeley, California

University of California
Los Angeles, California

University of California
Santa Barbara, California

University of Connecticut
Storrs, Connecticut

University of Florida
Gainesville, Florida

University of Georgia
Athens, Georgia

University of Illinois
Chicago, Illinois

University of Illinois
Urbana, Illinois

University of Iowa
Iowa City, Iowa

University of Kansas
Lawrence, Kansas

University of Maryland
College Park, Maryland

University of Miami
Miami, Florida

University of Michigan
Ann Arbor, Michigan

University of Minnesota
Minneapolis, Minnesota

University of Mississippi
University, Mississippi

University of Missouri
Columbia, Missouri

University of Nebraska
Lincoln, Nebraska

University of North Carolina
Chapel Hill, North Carolina

University of North Iowa
Cedar Falls, Iowa

University of the Pacific
Stockton, California

University of South Carolina
Columbia, South Carolina

University of South Dakota
Vermillion, South Dakota

University of Southern Florida
Tampa, Florida

University of Southern California
Los Angeles, California

University of Tennessee
Knoxville, Tennessee

University of Texas
Austin, Texas

University of Washington
Seattle, Washington

University of Wyoming
Laramie, Wyoming

Virginia Polytechnic Institute
Blacksburg, Virginia

Wayne State University
Detroit, Michigan

West Carolina University
Cullowhee, North Carolina

Western Michigan University
Kalamazoo, Michigan

Wichita State University
Wichita, Kansas

Appendix D. Colleges and Universities Offering Related Professional Education

Arizona State University, Tempe, Arizona
Auburn University, Auburn, Alabama
Boston College, Chestnut Hill, Massachusetts
Boston University, Boston, Massachusetts
Bradley University, Peoria, Illinois
Brigham Young University, Provo, Utah
California State College, Los Angeles, California
Catholic University, Washington, D.C.
Central Missouri State College, Warrensburg, Missouri
Chico State College, Chico, California
College of William and Mary, Williamsburg, Virginia
Colorado State University, Ft. Collins, Colorado
Columbia University, Teachers College, New York, New York
Eastern Washington State College, Cheney, Washington
Florida Atlantic University, Boca Raton, Florida
Florida State University, Tallahassee, Florida
George Washington University, Washington, D.C.
Illinois State University, Normal, Illinois
Indiana University, Bloomington, Indiana
Kansas State College, Ft. Hays, Kansas
Kansas State College, Pittsburg, Kansas
Kansas State Teachers College, Emporia, Kansas
Kansas State University, Manhattan, Kansas
Lehigh University, Bethlehem, Pennsylvania
Mankato State College, Mankato, Minnesota
Memphis State University, Memphis, Tennessee
Michigan State University, East Lansing, Michigan
Middle Tennessee State University, Murfreesboro, Tennessee
Mississippi State University, State College, Mississippi
Murray State University, Murray, Kentucky
Northern Arizona University, Flagstaff, Arizona
Northern Illinois University, DeKalb, Illinois
Oklahoma State University, Stillwater, Oklahoma
Oregon State University, Corvallis, Oregon
Purdue University, Lafayette, Indiana
Rhode Island College, Providence, Rhode Island
Rochester Institute of Technology, Rochester, New York
Sacramento State College, Sacramento, California
Sam Houston State College, Huntsville, Texas
San Diego State College, San Diego, California
San Jose State College, San Jose, California
Seattle University, Seattle, Washington
Southern Illinois University, Carbondale, Illinois
St. Louis University, St. Louis, Missouri
Stanford University, Palo Alto, California
State University of New York, Buffalo, New York

Stephen F. Austin State College, Nacogdoches, Texas
Texas Women's University, Denton, Texas
University of Arizona, Tucson, Arizona
University of California, Berkeley, California
University of California, Los Angeles, California
University of California, Santa Barbara, California
University of Colorado, Boulder, Colorado
University of Denver, Denver, Colorado
University of Florida, Gainesville, Florida
University of Georgia, Athens, Georgia
University of Hawaii, Honolulu, Hawaii
University of Illinois, Urbana, Illinois
University of Iowa, Iowa City, Iowa
University of Kansas, Lawrence, Kansas
University of Kentucky, Lexington, Kentucky
University of Louisville, Louisville, Kentucky
University of Maryland, College Park, Maryland
University of Miami, Coral Gables, Florida
University of Michigan, Ann Arbor, Michigan
University of Mississippi, University, Mississippi
University of Missouri, Columbia, Missouri
University of Nebraska, Lincoln, Nebraska
University of New Mexico, Albuquerque, New Mexico
University of North Carolina, Chapel Hill, North Carolina
University of Northern Iowa, Cedar Falls, Iowa
University of Oklahoma, Norman, Oklahoma
University of Oregon, Eugene, Oregon
University of Southern California, Los Angeles, California
University of South Dakota, Vermillion, South Dakota
University of South Florida, Tampa, Florida
University of Texas, Austin, Texas
University of Tulsa, Tulsa, Oklahoma
University of Virginia, Charlottesville, Virginia
University of Washington, Seattle, Washington
University of Wyoming, Laramie, Wyoming
Washington State University, Pullman, Washington
Wayne State University, Detroit, Michigan
Western Carolina University, Culowhee, North Carolina
Western Illinois University, Macomb, Illinois
Whitworth College, Spokane, Washington
Wichita State University, Wichita, Kansas

Appendix E. Programs For Professional Development of Community-Junior College Staff

During the 1970s, the demands on the American community-junior college may be the most vigorous of its history as a social institution. The diverse student body will demand that the educational promise of student-oriented, comprehensive programs be fulfilled. The staff of the community-junior college will be held primarily responsible for the success or failure of the college to keep its educational promise. Since community-junior colleges emphasize teaching, the faculty chiefly will carry the burden of response to the demands of society, community, and the student for meaningful educational programs and relationships.

The preparation of the staff will determine, to a great extent, the ability of the college to satisfy the demands for quality education in the 1970s. This section examines the numbers and types of preservice and inservice education programs which are available to community-junior college staff today.

Unfortunately, many of these programs — especially those for faculty — are underdeveloped. Kelly and Connolly [1970] say that present community-junior college preservice programs can place less than 150 faculty each year. Phair [1968] reports that California faculty preservice programs produced only 47 and 49 new community-junior college candidates in 1968 and 1969, respectively. Programs for administrators are somewhat better developed but still not adequate to the needs for the preparation of community-junior college staff.

The lack of adequate numbers of special preparation programs means that community-junior college staff are being educated elsewhere. Of course, this section cannot describe the preparation programs aimed at staffs of other kinds of colleges. However, the author does assume that more and more proposed special staff preparation programs will come into existence during the 70s. Many of these proposed programs are described in this section.

The section is divided into two major parts — preservice and inservice programs. Within each major part, programs for administrators, faculty and professional services staff are discussed. In some cases, programs offer both preservice and inservice education. Such programs are listed under both categories whenever possible; otherwise, the preservice or inservice emphasis of the general program determines its categorization.

For the purposes of this report, preservice program discussions are limited to those educational experiences leading to a degree and employment in a community college. Inservice education programs are to be considered as those professional development experiences provided to staff members after they have been employed by a college.

The section does not pretend to be an exhaustive survey or a handbook for planners. Nevertheless, within its limitations it should be a help to those who plan staff development programs.

PRESERVICE PROGRAMS
Administrators

The problem of professional development for community college administrators has not gone completely unaddressed. Since the early 1960s, preservice development programs for community-junior college administrators have been receiving increasing attention and financial support. Universities throughout the country have undertaken preservice preparation of administrators through the development of doctoral programs in higher education specializing in junior college administration or the establishment of supervised internships with cooperating community-junior colleges or both.

Two major sources of funds have advanced administrator preservice preparation programs to the fore of all community-junior college staff development programs. The W. K. Kellogg Foundation has funded Junior College Leadership centers and fellowships throughout the nation. The U.S. Office of Education has established graduate fellowship programs for community-junior college staff members through Part E of the Education Professions Development Act.

The Junior College Leadership Programs

To date, the greatest effort aimed at preparing and training community-junior college administrators has been performed under the aegis of the Junior College Leadership Program. This program, which has been funded since 1959 by the W. K. Kellogg Foundation in cooperation with the American Association of Junior Colleges and participating universities, is an outgrowth of the Foundation's successful experience in supporting administrative leadership training at the elementary and secondary school level. In conjunction with the A.A.J.C.'s Commission of Administration, the Foundation has supported the establishment of regional administrative training centers at participating universities throughout the country.

At present, eleven universities in seven states participate as Kellogg centers. The universities are: the University of California at Los Angeles, the University of California at Berkeley, the University of Colorado,

Columbia University, the University of Florida, Florida State University, the University of Michigan, Michigan State University, Wayne State University, the University of Washington and the University of Texas.

The participating universities have undertaken the following major preservice preparation tasks:

(1) the development of techniques by which administrators can be identified, selected, and recruited;

(2) experimentation in the approaches used to prepare and improve potential and practicing community college administrators;

(3) the offering of doctoral and master's level programs covering educational administration, social and philosophical foundations, psychological foundations, guidance and student personnel services, curriculum and instruction.

Of course, there has been considerable latitude in the development of programs. Universities have attempted to integrate their special facilities or interests into the Kellogg programs. For example, the U.C.L.A. Leadership Program emphasizes administrative innovation. Program participants also use the ERIC Clearinghouse for Junior Colleges, which is housed on the U.C.L.A. campus. Berkeley is renowned for its Center for Research and Development in Higher Education; its junior college leadership program participants are expected to show expertise in statistics and research methodology.

Each of the participating universities offers a doctoral program with specialization in community-junior college administration. Each institution receives direct financial support from the Kellogg Foundation for the establishment of a center and fellowships for students. [Johnson, 1964.] This financial assistance from the Kellogg Foundation has enabled the eleven participating universities to produce the lion's share of doctorates, course offerings, and research publications in community-junior college administration.

EPDA Fellowship Programs

Part E of the Education Professions Development Act has provided funds to assist colleges and universities in meeting critical shortages of highly qualified personnel who are serving or are preparing to serve as teachers, administrators, or educational specialists in institutions of higher education. The first grants approved under this program in 1969 included $2.2 million for 421 one- and two-year fellowship grants, as well as $4.7 million for training some 4000 participants in 78 short courses and workshops.

For 1971–72, the Office of Education has approved 903 fellowships to graduate students who participate in 91 selected programs. Fellowship programs are conducted in 80 colleges and universities located in 41 states and the District of Columbia. The total cost of these programs is five million dollars.

In 1971, 151 institutions submitted 233 program proposals for 3279 fellowships to the U.S. Office of Education. These proposals were screened by panels of independent professional consultants from various colleges and universities. These consultants recommended the final programs to be funded by the Office of Education.

Among other qualifications, a person is eligible for an EPDA fellowship nomination if he has been accepted for full-time graduate study in an approved program at the nominating institution of higher education. Administrators and educational specialists are eligible at both the master's and doctoral levels.

More than 70 percent of the 1971–72 EPDA fellowship programs were for the development of community-junior college personnel. Thus, in 1971–72, there were 54 programs and 557 fellowships for the development of these personnel. In addition to these fellowships, there were 31 programs with a total number of 263 fellowships for two- and four-year personnel. Since it is not possible to determine how these latter fellowships were allocated (for two- or four-year trainees) they will all be considered together in the following review.

Of the total eighty-five community-junior college staff development programs, 2 programs with 17 fellowships were offered for faculty and administration; 9 programs with 68 fellowships were offered for administrators; and 1 program was offered with 7 fellowships for administrators and educational specialists. Included in the educational specialists' category were student personnel workers, counselors, and others.

Other Programs

As stated previously, most community-junior college staff members are enrolled in preservice programs which are not designed for their professional needs. Schultz [1969] corroborates this generalization for chief community-junior college administrators. Schultz reports that as late as 1967, nearly 45 percent of all newly-appointed presidents of community-junior colleges did not possess doctoral degrees. Of those with doctorates, few had specialized preparation in community-junior college administration. A substantial number of presidents had been recruited from elementary and secondary school positions and nearly half the presidents appointed from 1952 to 1967 had had neither formal study of the junior colleges nor experience as a teacher or administrator in such an institution.

This section cannot describe in detail the lack of preparation programs for community-junior college administrators, but it can and does suggest that the absence of such programs is the rule rather than the exception. There are, however, some other preservice programs, of which two are described next.

North Carolina State University offers a doctoral program in community-junior college administration which is not part of the Junior College Leadership or the EPDA fellowship programs. This program is sponsored by the Department of Adult Education at the University in cooperation with the State Board of Higher Education and the 43 local community colleges. It is based upon a four-step education program stressing actual experience. A program of interdisciplinary coursework, inservice educational experience, practical field experience and a major research project constitute the degree requirements [Adams, 1967].

The coursework includes such topics as: The Comprehensive Community College, Principles of Adult Learning, Program Planning, Curriculum Development, Organization and Administration, Public School Law, and Public School Financing and Budgeting. Additional coursework draws upon Sociology, Anthropology, Political Science, Economics, Psychology, and Philosophy. Special seminars are also presented to acquaint candidates with new developments in community college education. Heavy emphasis is placed upon previous administrative experience and ongoing administrative performance in internship and field experience assignments.

North Carolina State's program may exemplify other administrator preparation programs that are not funded by the Kellogg Foundation or the U.S. Office of Education. The next program to be discussed shows the potential direction of preservice preparation for a particular segment of community college administrators. Whereas the Kellogg programs prepare mostly presidents and academic officers, this program has attempted to prepare chief student personnel administrators for the community-junior college.

In 1968–69, a National Defense Education Act Grant was given to the University of Illinois for a preservice program for four-year and two-year college administrators of student personnel services. The program was based on a study by O'Banion [1966] which indicated that a core of experiences should be common to all college and university student personnel workers. The suggested common core included courses of psychology, counseling, an overview of student personnel work, higher education, the study of the college student, sociology and anthropology, and a practicum in student personnel work.

The University of Illinois program incorporated many of O'Banion's suggestions. The program goals and objectives were to prepare graduates for positions of major decision-making authority in higher education; to broaden, deepen, and supplement the student's previous experiences through field observation and practice; to provide firsthand views of philosophies, policies, roles, procedures and functions of some selected student personnel administrators at all levels of higher education; to familiarize the students with the literature of the profession; and to increase the student's knowledge and competency in an area of special relevance to him through internship.

The core coursework of this program included: The American College, The Junior College, The College Student, Interdisciplinary Foundations of Student Personnel Administration, Group Dynamics and Leadership, Organization and Administration of Student Personnel Work in Higher Education, Research Problems in Higher Education, and an Internship in a variety of educational environments.

Half of the students in the Institute planned to gain employment at community-junior colleges. Internships at community-junior colleges and special seminars on student personnel work in the community-junior college were provided.

The Illinois preservice program was classed as an N.D.E.A.-sponsored Institute. The N.D.E.A. later became incorporated in the E.P.D.A. The E.P.D.A. also sponsors institutes which could be classified as preservice preparation experiences for administrators and other staff. The importance of these institutes as preservice education opportunities should not be underestimated. However, since E.P.D.A. institutes are one-year maximum experiences for participants and since these institutes do not necessarily require participant admission to an approved graduate program of the sponsoring college or university, they are primarily classified as inservice education experiences for the purposes of this report.

Internship Experiences

The graduate student internship has long been a cornerstone of the strong preservice programs for community-junior college administrators. Illinois, North Carolina State and many E.P.D.A. fellowship program institutions offer internships as part of their preservice education programs.

But the internship experience is most often remembered as a chief strength of the Kellogg programs. In fact, the preservice internship experience for community-junior college administrators emerged from Kellogg-sponsored elementary and secondary school administrator internships and preservice programs [Kellogg, 1961]. The Kellogg Foundation has stated:

The chief objectives of internship in educational administration are to help the intern develop a more comprehensive view of educational administration, to provide him with the experience of real administrative responsibility, and to enable him to benefit from lessons learned by the sponsoring administrator during his professional experience. It has also been found, that interns have provided many useful services to sponsoring administrators. . . . [Kellogg, 1961.]

The Kellogg-sponsored University of California at Los Angeles Leadership Program offers an excellent example of some long-range benefits to community-junior colleges which accrue from graduate internships. UCLA has had 54 students serve as community college interns. Of this group, 43 are currently in community-junior college positions, 37 of which are administrative in nature. Six former interns are now serving as presidents, and 17 are presently vice president or deans of community-junior colleges [Johnson, 1971].

Most internship programs are designed to provide each student with that community college exposure which is commensurate with his occupational interests and academic work. Under the guidance of a university faculty member and a community college administrator, the student is given appropriate assignments. Interns may serve on a full-time basis for a year or a semester, or on a part-time basis for longer periods of time. Some interns are supported by fellowship grants from the Kellogg Foundation, while others receive an appropriate salary from their host college.

The administrative assignments given to interns vary. Johnson [1963] states that interns usually participate in meetings of the college's central administrative bodies, such as the board of trustees and the administrative council of the president and deans. Other typical intern experiences are service as an assistant to the president; participation in budget preparation; planning curriculum changes; participation in the development of educational policies and administrative procedures; participation in institutional research projects; service as an assistant to a dean or other administrator; and work with lay advisory committees.

The educational value of internship programs also varies among institutions. McCuen [1965] states that some community-junior colleges relegate interns to observer roles while others disregard the intern's education while asking him to solve many of their institution's problems.

If internships are to be effective educational experiences, then several dimensions must be present. The Midwest Community College Leadership Program — under the auspices of Michigan, Michigan State, and Wayne State Universities — requires the following dimensions:

(1) The intern must be anxious to work and willing to learn. The intern himself must help determine the kinds of experiences which he is seeking.

(2) The host college must be well-run and possess a good staff of administrators.

(3) The intern must receive salary commensurate with his contribution and there must be adequate supervision on a regular basis.

(4) The intern must be matched to the position, and the faculty advisor must work closely with the intern and the host administrator to bring the field experience to fulfillment. [Hall, 1963.]

Although there are often difficulties in finding enough suitable intern positions at community colleges, the impact of the internship programs has been significant. At the minimum, the internship phase of preservice administrator education has helped to assure that the preservice programs of universities and the expectations of potential administrators are realistic in terms of the actual problems and the activities with which community-junior colleges are concerned. Additionally, the opportunity to engage in assignments in a real world environment has proven of benefit to both the intern and the college and has enhanced the relevance of preservice administrator development programs. Overall, it would appear that the internship is a highly valued form of preservice education and that its use is likely to continue on a widespread basis.

Faculty

The state of preservice education opportunities for faculty is more anticipatory than realized at present. There is a dearth of specific programs available for prospective faculty in 1971, but an abundance of diverse offerings may be available in the future.

Present Programs and Courses

The American Association of Junior Colleges [*Preservice,* 1969] has issued a statement expressing deep concern with the graduate education now available for those persons contemplating a career commitment as a faculty member in a community-junior college. Gleazer in 1965 notes that over the past several years the A.A.J.C., through its Commission on Instruction, has urged the establishment of university-centered programs to recruit and prepare community-junior college instructors. The Association's efforts have been based on the assump-

tions that (1) there is an urgent need for great numbers of academic and
occupational faculty and (2) specialized programs of recruitment and
preparation are necessary for the quality education of community-junior
college students.

In 1969, the Association listed 75 to 100 graduate institutions
offering identifiable graduate programs designed to prepare new community-junior college faculty in one or more recognized disciplines.
(Appendix C.) These institutions awarded M.A., M.S., Ph.D. and Ed.D.
degrees for the successful completion of their preservice programs. The
A.A.J.C. list did not include institutions which offered occasional courses
about the community-junior college; it surveyed only specific degree-
preparation programs.

In 1970, Smolich surveyed universities to determine the current
status and anticipated growth of professional education courses and programs offered by schools of education which were specific to the topic
of the two-year college. Important, too, was the extent and anticipated
growth in student enrollment in these courses. The survey was prompted
by a concern for the professional preparation of two-year college staff
members in response to the explosive growth in student enrollments.

Although the Smolich survey includes courses and programs for
administrators and special services staff, the survey is mentioned only in
this section. The reasons for this singular inclusion are based on the
results of the survey, the inability to separate adequately the student-
to-be-administrator from the student-to-be-instructor in courses; and the
desire to minimize reader confusion.

Eighty-two institutions responded to the Smolich survey. In addition, Smolich included 5 nonresponding institutions in his results because
of their known preparation programs for two-year college staff members.
The total 87 institutions are included in Appendix D.

Geographically the 87 institutions are located in 34 states. Forty-
one percent of the institutions are located in 6 states (California, 9; Illinois, 6; Kansas, 6; Florida, 5; Washington, 5; Texas, 4). As could be
expected, these states are among the leaders in community-junior college
development. Several general categories were established (Table 1) for the
course titles provided by the 82 responding institutions. Courses specific
to the two-year college are listed separately from those relating to the
broader topic of higher education. Courses in the latter category include
some content relating to the two-year college and are, therefore, included
in the data presented.

By far the most popular category is the "general overview course."
This category and the next three course title categories (curriculum,
methods and procedures of instruction, and teaching internship) provide

APPENDIX E — TABLE 1

General Categories of Professional Education Courses Relating to the Two-year College in 82 Schools of Education 1969–70

	Number of Course Titles	
Course Title Categories	Two-Year College	Higher Education
General overview course	69	19
Curricular areas	(37)	(9)
General curriculum	19	8
Occupational	6	1
Adult education	3	0
Specific subject areas	6	0
Other	3	0
Methods and Procedures of Instruction	31	9
Internship	21	0
Administration	19	19
Student services	11	7
Research	3	2
Students	1	6

the core for current preparation programs for two-year college instructors.

During 1969–70, the 82 responding institutions enrolled 10,107 students in 307 courses. (Table 2.) By 1972–73, course offerings should jump by 27 percent to 384; student numbers should increase 56 percent to 15,769.

Seven institutions (Universities of Washington, Florida, Missouri; Florida State University; Northern Illinois University; California State College at Los Angeles; and Auburn University) — all with over 300 total course enrollments — accounted for 28 percent of the total 1969–70 student enrollment. The University of Washington led the 82 institutions with total course enrollments of 550. (Table 3.)

APPENDIX E — TABLE 2

Summary Data of 82 Responding Institutions Offering Professional Education Courses/Programs Relating to the Two-year College

Course Titles			Enrollment		
1966–67	1969–70	Est. 1972–73	1969–70	Est. 1972–73	Percent Increase
186	307	384	10,107	15,769	56
Degrees: Specialty in the Two-Year College					
MA 37		Certificate 15		Dr. 45	None 15

Developmental Data of Sixteen Institutions With Enrollment Projections of 250 and Over in Professional Education Courses/Programs Specific to the Two-year College

1972–73 Academic Year

Institution	Course Titles			Enrollment			Degrees: Specialty in J.C.		
	1966–67	1969–70	Est. 1972–73	1969–70	1972–73	Projected % Change	MA	Certificate	Dr.
University of Washington	6	7	9	550	800	+ 45	X		X
University of Florida	8	11	11	455	715	+ 57	X	X	X
Florida State University	5	7	7	360	680	+ 89	X		X
Auburn University	3	7	7	315	610	+ 94	X	X	X
Oregon State University	3	3	7	167	510	+205	X		X
Northern Illinois University	5	6	8	414	414	0	X	X	X
Arizona State University	4	8	8	291	359	+ 23			X
Brigham Young University	3	4	6	255	355	+ 39			X
University of Hawaii	0	6	10	139	350	+159		X*	X*
San Jose State College	3	3	3	260	325	+ 25	X**		
Michigan State University	4	5	6	245	323	+ 32	X	X	X
Washington State University	3	6	6	233	310	+ 33	X		X
California State College (LA)	3	4	4	300	300	0	X**		
Illinois State University	6	6	7	185	265	+ 43	X	X	X
University of Missouri	1	6	6	320	260	− 19			X
University of Oklahoma	4	4	5	188	250	+ 33			X
TOTALS	61	93	110	4,677	6,826	+ 46			

*In planning stage
**In teaching area only

Projected enrollments for the 1972–73 academic year indicate considerable growth and increased emphasis upon two-year college staff preparation at many institutions. The sixteen institutions projecting enrollments of 250 or more are listed in Table 3.   Notable in the list is the University of Washington which expects an enrollment of over 800, largest expected enrollment of the 82 institutions. Oregon State University expects a 205 percent increase. These sixteen institutions (of the 82 responding) accounted for almost half the 1969–70 student enrollment in courses specific to the two-year college and, based on current projections, will account for 43 percent of enrollments in 1972–73.

The casual observer might consider these enrollments in 87 institutions to be adequate to the needs of community-junior colleges. However, such an observation is incorrect for several reasons. First, not all the students in all the courses expect to become staff members in the community-junior college. Even if a student expects such employment, he may not take it upon graduation. Second, the institutions report each student in each course in their total figures. Thus, one student taking four courses is counted as four students at a responding institution in the Smolich study. Third, the total of 87 institutions is only about one-twentieth of the total 1600 four-year colleges and universities in the nation. Finally, the fact that 41 percent of the responding institutions are located in six states indicates that the other forty-four states with community-junior colleges are not receiving an even distribution of the opportunities and advantages of this education.

New Directions

The reform of graduate education programs for community-junior college faculty has taken two basic directions. The first direction maintains the traditional graduate degree but changes some of the education experiences which are necessary to attain that degree. The second direction changes both the degree and the program in an attempt to escape academic "traditionalism" in the graduate education experiences. More degree options are created in this latter attempt and at least one major advisory council, The Carnegie Commission on Higher Education [1971], states that a trend toward more degree options will continue in the foreseeable future.

The major focus of both reform attempts has been the reorientation of graduate programs from research-scholarship to teaching-scholarship. Wortham [1967] notes the benefits which would accrue to community colleges if they would focus their efforts on finding teaching-oriented programs from the doctoral level on down:

(1) The standards of teaching and quality of instruction would tend to rise. The availability of the teaching degrees at higher levels would tend to exert an upward pressure in the area of teacher preparation.

(2) More community-junior college instructors would pursue advanced degrees, thereby lending both greater depth and breadth to the educational level of teaching facilities. Eventually, a larger proportion of the most highly trained teachers would be at the service of the greatest number of college students.

(3) A greater number of teachers would be equipped to attack the serious accumulation of problems in curriculum and instruction in the two-year college.

(4) The equivalency of transfer work and articulation with four-year colleges would improve along with the depth of vocational curricula.

(5) The teaching-oriented doctorate (Ph.D. or D.A.T.) and other degrees would recognize that college teaching is no less worthy of professional preparation than research, in conjunction with scholarship. Personal aspirations of faculty would be open to greater satisfaction.

The previously-mentioned faculty preparation programs at 75–87 colleges and universities are basic attempts to orient graduate education to the needs of two-year college teachers. The following have been suggested as improvements to these present programs. The first suggestions maintain the traditional degree; the second are new degree programs.

Improvement of Traditional Degree-Granting Programs

This section discusses some present and proposed improvements for faculty preservice education in programs which offer traditional academic degrees. The section considers some model EPDA programs and a proposal for the establishment of semi-autonomous university centers for the preparation of community-junior college teachers. In all of these model programs, the internship is stressed as a basic educational experience for the students.

In 1971–72, 60 EPDA fellowship programs with 585 fellowships were offered for teachers; two programs with 17 fellowships were offered for faculty and administration; 11 programs with 151 fellowships were offered for teachers and educational specialists. In total, 70 percent of the community-junior college EPDA fellowship programs were for the preparation of teachers in academic areas.

At the University of Arizona, seven new and five continuing students are preparing to teach English in community-junior colleges. At the end of two years and an intervening summer session, the students receive an M.A. in English and are prepared for an Arizona Junior College Certificate. The students receive special education which concerns community-junior colleges. They participate in internships which focus upon the development of cross-discipline approaches to instruction. In conjunction with internships in literature and composition, the candidates observe senior English classes in a local high school.

The University of Hawaii offers EPDA fellowships to students who possess bachelor's or master's degrees in a subject field, meet college admission requirements, provide notice from a junior college official regarding tentative assurance of positions, and are not currently teaching in two-year, post-high school institutions.

The program of study lasts for two years and a summer session; it is divided into three phases. The first phase consists of academic preparation in a major subject field which leads to a master's degree or its equivalent. This requires the completion of 30–36 credits, six of which are in professional education courses. Phase two consists of a core of community college foundation courses. This involves an acquaintance with the history and philosophy of junior colleges, organization and administration, evaluation, curriculum, audio-visual media, community college teaching, vocational education, and learning theory. In phase three, a fellow serves an internship at one of the three community colleges on the island, where he teaches a minimum of three courses. During this time he is assisted by a cooperating teacher who counsels him, evaluates his internship performance, arranges two hours of work per week through the Dean of Student Service to enable the fellow to acquire familiarity with student service functions and procedures, helps the intern establish necessary contacts, arranges for him to observe several different types of classes, approves and coordinates the intern's required project in community or student services or both, arranges for the student to attend various administrative meetings and conferences, and meets and confers with the seminar leader (seminars are held concurrently with the internship). After he completes phase three, the EPDA fellow is tentatively awarded an advanced certificate degree.

Previously, this report mentioned an NDEA institute at the University of Illinois which was designed as a preservice administrator education program despite its moderate length — one year — and its non-requirement of participant admission in an approved graduate program at the University. The E.P.D.A. Institute can also serve as a preservice education experience for faculty despite its preponderant use in inservice education. The following example discusses just one of many such institutes which can offer the same program as preservice and inservice education for community-junior college faculty.

Texas Tech University has initiated an Institute for Preservice Training of Junior College Teachers which is held during summer sessions and followed by an internship in the fall. The program assumes that the participant has a master's degree in the discipline he wishes to teach. The Institute lasts for six weeks, during which the participant takes two three-credit courses in the morning: Curriculum and Instruction in the Junior College and Seminar in Higher Education. During the afternoon, the participant attends a workshop devoted to the development of materials for a course which he expects to teach in the fall. Orientation visits to junior colleges are also included in the workshop activities.

In the fall, when the participant is on his first full-time teaching assignment, he begins an internship which is considered an integral part of the Institute program. Texas Tech University professors observe the teaching participant in his classroom. These professors help the teacher-student to evaluate his effectiveness in the classroom. The professors also offer interdisciplinary seminars for participants in the fall. The internship carries three semester hours of credit.

The E.P.D.A. fellowship programs and institutes are operating throughout the country. Many of these programs offer the core course experiences which were described by Smolich plus a strong internship for the program participants.

In 1970, as a result of a research study funded by the U.S. Office of Education, Cohen [1970] proposed the establishment of new graduate centers for the systematic preparation of community-junior college teachers. These centers would also offer core courses as well as strong internship experiences. The educational experiences would lead to the traditional B.A. or B.S., the M.A. or M.S., or doctor of philosophy degree but with the master's degree as the usual terminal degree. Multiple entry and exit points would be allowed with the earliest entry starting in an undergraduate's junior year so that prospective faculty can be exposed much earlier to the strategies, techniques and subject matter orientations considered desirable for junior college instruction.

The preparatory sequence at the master's level would consist of 32 semester credits the first year. The second year would comprise a supervised professional internship and related activities to strengthen the candidate's teaching competency.

The internship would constitute the culmination of the teaching learning process material offered by the centers of the master's level. The centers and the employer community-junior colleges would accept joint responsibility for insuring the success of the internship. The internship would require the teaching of only two sections of one course per week. This limitation is intended to permit intern participation in case study workshops and small group seminars back at the center, and observation and participation at the college where the intern is assigned. Collateral activities would consist of fifteen class hours of observation of other teacher activities and orientation to the college's personnel services, learning resource centers, developmental programs, community services, career occupational programs, and governance and administrative practices.

The centers proposal and the EPDA programs are not the only preservice education opportunities for faculty which attempt to offer new experiences, especially internships, to graduate students. There are others, important others, such as the joint St. Louis Junior College District and Southern Illinois master's degree program with internship. This program has received $500,000 from the Ford Foundation as an incentive to its efforts to increase the supply of effective community-junior college teachers. Also, Case [1970] reports that a Cooperative Internship Program (CIP) has been jointly planned by a team of community college University of California personnel. By coordinating the resources of the cooperating community colleges, the University, and the U.S. Office of Education, the CIP will offer a two-week preservice institute which provides an intensive introduction to the community college, curriculum development, instructional strategies, students and student characteristics. Then interns will teach a 70 percent load for the academic year under the guidance of an outstanding instructor at the college.

The New Degree-Granting Programs

Some universities believe that the name as well as the preservice program must be changed if the new teaching orientation of graduate programs is to be made clear to students and employer community-junior colleges. This decision to change graduate program degree titles has caused considerable debate among the planners of these preservice programs. The controversy has centered on the doctorate level titles — D.A.T. (doctor of arts in teaching) or Ph.D.

Proponents for the change of name argue that Ph.D.'s produce most internal ills of our colleges, i.e. student alienation, irrelevant curricula, uninspired teaching, outmoded traditions, and unnecessary specialization of undergraduate teaching [Dunham, 1970]; Ph.D.'s are in oversupply and ill-equipped to accept employment in the community-junior college market; therefore, a teaching doctorate of equal rigor and prestige, the doctor of arts in teaching, should be developed to prepare teachers for the market.

Connolly [1971] notes the close relationship among community colleges, Ph.D.'s and the educational marketplace. He feels the current Ph.D. surplus could benefit the community-junior college by forcing graduate schools to reassess their goals and programs. Moreover, it could result in innovative and effective programs for developing community-junior college faculty. However, the surplus also has the potential to change the concept of the open-door community college. It remains to be seen whether those hiring faculty in the two-year college can resist the temptation to "enhance" their staff by adding Ph.D.'s, and if not, whether the community-junior college can assimilate many individuals who may reject the institution's basic philosophy.

Opponents of the doctor of arts in teaching degree have strongly attacked the basic assumptions of the proposal. Most of the controversy swirls around comparison of the D.A.T. with the previously-established Ph.D. To the contention that Ph.D.'s have generated most of the internal ills of colleges, defenders reply that it is not the Ph.D., but the educators who specify Ph.D. requirements and proposals who have erred. They maintain that the Ph.D. can still be the degree offered in all fields to mark scholarly individuals.

The present oversupply of Ph.D.'s is not considered disastrous because it is thought they will replace less-qualified personnel in areas where Ph.D.'s previously did not accept positions. In a survey of plans for the Carnegie Commission on Higher Education, Mayhew [1970] stated that given the continued respect in which the Ph.D. is held in comparison with other types of doctorates, this phenomenon of surplus is likely to foreclose any widespread adoption of special kinds of doctoral programs for the preparation of college teachers unless the expanding capacity of graduate training is modified for such a purpose.

To many individuals and institutions the D.A.T. is a "cheap" doctorate incapable of garnering the prestige and respect of the Ph.D. If a D.A.T. is to be equally as rigorous as the Ph.D., and, consequently, as costly in institutional and human resources, why not offer a Ph.D. modified toward teaching in the community-junior college? In fact, the Carnegie Commission on Higher Education [1971] recommended that the time required to earn a B.A. be shortened by one year and the time required to earn a Ph.D. be shortened by one or two years. Mayhew [1970] supports the observation concerning the less-than-enthusiastic reception the D.A.T. is receiving when he states that campus visits to 111 institutions showed the new teaching doctorate did not reveal widespread, active interest.

Regardless of the eventual resolution of this verbal tug-of-war, both proponents and opponents of the change-of-degree name concur that the graduate program emphasis should turn from research to teaching. The controversy concerns the way in which that turning should take place.

The proponents of name-change have drawn some strong allies to their cause. At the master's level, the Committee on Preparation of Junior

College Teachers, *Master Plan Phase III of the Illinois State Board of Higher Education,* [1969] has recommended a new degree program for the preservice education of community-junior college teachers of liberal arts and general education subjects:

(1) The degree should be designated as the Master of Arts or Master of Science in College Teaching or Specialist in College Teaching. The new designation will identify the variety of specific programs subsumed under it, and it will also indicate the special purpose of the degree.

(2) The program should have a core of subjects identified with recognized disciplines, i.e., English, biology, mathematics, etc. equivalent to or exceeding the academic standards of the Master of Arts or Master of Science. We emphasize this point on behalf of the junior college student, especially the transfer student, who must have this kind of knowledge to complete his last two years.

(3) The program should include options outside of the basic disciplines. This will enable the prospective teacher to acquire a breadth of knowledge that will prepare him for teaching in an institution in which the degree of specialization is much less than it is in the universities.

(4) The program should normally include a supervised teaching experience as a part of the academic program. We recommend that the teaching experience be obtained in the degree-granting institution and/or in cooperation with the junior college.

(5) The program should include a seminar on the institutions of higher education with appropriate attention to the junior college. The point of this requirement is to acquaint the student with the nature of the institution in which he will work and more broadly with the nature of higher education in America.

(6) The program should be considered terminal, in the sense that its successful completion qualifies the student to teach in the junior college. At the same time, the program should be such that students with a variety of educational backgrounds should be able to enter it. Finally, the program should be so designated that students, in their quest for self-improvement, can enter doctoral programs in the same area of study.

This proposed degree program offers the coursework and internship experiences which characterize some of the major innovative — but traditional degree granting — programs in the nation. The degree requires two years of graduate study, but the Illinois State Board Committee believes that programming should be flexible enough to permit capable students to complete the degree in a shorter time.

At the intermediate level of degree programs, graduates have traditionally been awarded with advanced certificates, specialist degrees, or the famous, informal, all-but-dissertation degrees. The advocates of title change believe that this level of educational accomplishment should be represented by the doctor of philosophy (D. Phil.) or diploma in college teaching (D.C.T. degree). Organized to incorporate post-master's academic and experiential training, these programs increase teaching skill and broad-based disciplinary mastery in primary or allied subject fields. Again there is danger that the teaching orientation may be lost. Degrees such as the candidate in philosophy (Cand. Phil.) and Yale's master of philosophy (M. Phil.) are discounted for community-junior colleges since they primarily serve to mark the pre-dissertation stage of a Ph.D. program which is often void of the teaching skills emphasis [Cardozier, 1968].

The National Faculty Association of Community and Junior Colleges has offered guidelines for the establishment of an interim degree program which assumes that the student holds a master's degree in a subject area. The program degree referred to is the candidate degree in college teaching. It consists of an additional 30+ semester hours of credit within the subject area. Such study would consist of combinations of subject area courses and appropriate interdisciplinary subject area courses. If the student, in his master's work, has not completed the modules of history, philosophy, and function of the community-junior college within the field of higher education and special problems in the subject area, then these requirements must be met as a requisite of the candidate's degree. At the termination of this period of study, the student normally will have spent six years in preparation and must pass comprehensive examinations comparable to those given to Ph.D. candidates.

In order to complete the requirements for the candidate's degree, the student would then complete work in the areas of leadership problems in community-junior colleges, including professional and legal concerns, legislation, administration, and finances; education research and testing; and characteristics of students, including learning theory, psychology, educational sociology, student advisement, counseling, and/or guidance.

A nine-credit hour, one-semester, full-time internship in community-junior college teaching, with full compensation for the intern while teaching, must be taken concurrently with a continuing one-semester Intern Seminar in Community-Junior College Teaching, for which three hours of credit will be granted. It is intended and expected that the period of internship, coupled with the later one-year residency, will be a time of introspective teaching under the guidance of fully qualified professionals at the host institution.

Miami-Dade Junior College and the University of Miami co-sponsor a diploma in a college-teaching program. The diploma in collegiate teaching is designed so that a graduate can teach interdisciplinary courses in his general area of knowledge as well as basic courses in his discipline. It is also designed to help the graduate attain a grasp of research results and the ability to communicate them to others. The program includes a minimum of forty hours in the student's major and related fields, eight hours of electives and twelve hours in professional education courses which consist of an internship in community college teaching as well as courses in the nature of students, instruction, and the community college. During his final semester, the student participates in an interdisciplinary seminar. At this time he makes a course presentation to be criticized by his peers and instructors, or takes a comprehensive examination, or both.

While there has been some controversy over these "new" lower level degrees, the greatest debate has been at the highest level — the doctorate. The doctor of arts-in-teaching concept is not new. Strothman [1955] wrote on behalf of a committee of fifteen that there should be a new doctor's degree, not less rigorous, but different. The training for this degree should be oriented toward preparing men and women to teach effectively in college.

The Illinois State Board Committee recommends a new doctor of arts in teaching program for community-junior college faculty in which:

(1) All programs should be designed to enable the full-time student to finish in three and not more than four years after he has obtained his baccalaureate.

(2) The substance of the new doctorate should include major subject-matter areas, but it should also include courses related to the functions of college teaching. These are an integral part of the junior college environment and vitally important in the light of the legal requirement to admit students of widely varying backgrounds and precollege achievement. We must make every effort to enable students of such widely differing competencies to begin and to finish the educational programs best suited to them.

(3) The program of preparation should emphasize the interrelatedness of subject matter, as the curriculum should be designed to insure this emphasis.

(4) The program should include an investigation that could concentrate, as an example, on the problem of education in specific kinds of environment, i.e., rural, urban, social and economic, etc. This investigation could well concentrate on the problems teachers face in the junior college and, for that matter, on the almost kaleidoscope problems the institution itself faces.

(5) The program should normally include a supervised teaching experience, and this may be best accomplished by a term or a semester of teaching in either the junior or the senior institution. Interinstitutional arrangements for this should be flexible, so that the student is not unduly restricted in his choices, but also formal enough to maintain adequate supervision of the student.

(6) The program should emphasize the student's competence in subject areas.

Two national groups add strength to this state support of the D.A.T. degree program. The Carnegie Corporation offers the advisory and financial power of an interested bystander while the National Faculty Association of Community and Junior Colleges offers support from the center of concern — the faculty themselves.

The Carnegie Commission on Higher Education [1971] has recommended that the doctor of arts in teaching degree be encouraged and become fully accepted. The Commission has also recommended that a specified number of fellowships be made available each year to students in the programs.

Koenker [1971] stated that sixty-eight institutions are either launch- . ing, developing or considering D.A.T. programs to prepare community-junior college or college teachers. In 1970, three institutions offered the doctor of arts in teaching — Carnegie-Mellon and the Universities of North Dakota and Oregon. Twenty-seven additional institutions offered a sixth-year program for preparing community-junior college or college teachers. That same year, the Carnegie Corporation granted $935,000 to ten institutions for the new degree in 1970: Dartmouth College, Brown University, Massachusetts Institute of Technology, State University of New York at Albany, Ball State University, University of Michigan, Idaho State University, University of Washington, Washington State University, and the Claremont University Center. These programs were expected to be in operation by 1971 [Dunham, 1970].

Idaho State University's 1971 graduate catalog describes one of these Carnegie Corporation-sponsored D.A.T. programs:

The Doctor of Arts (in teaching) is a terminal degree sponsored by departments within the College of Liberal Arts under supervision of the Graduate School. Degree programs vary according to the needs of individual disciplines, but all programs share common features judged effective in producing qualified undergraduate and community college instructors, among these: high entrance and candidacy requirements, broad rather than specialized training, flexible curricula, attention to trends in higher education, and supervised teaching internships. Applicants for degree programs should be reasonably certain that they also possess those qualities of mind and temperament which are compatible with the demands of such instruction.

The National Faculty Association recommends that the doctor of arts in teaching degree program should include all of the requirements of the proposed candidate in college teaching program. In addition, the student will undertake an academic year of full-time teaching in a community-junior college with full remuneration. After this one-year professional residency, he will participate in a Post-Teaching Evaluation Seminar which consists of a critical evaluation of a written log and terminal report and the oral doctoral examination by the candidate's doctoral committee. The written log and terminal report must show evidence of successful performance during the full-time teaching assignment, e.g., a description of innovative teaching practices; a log of teaching experience; course syllabi; evaluations of the candidate by supervisors and administrators; recordings and video-tapes of teaching performance. The oral examination provides the D.A.T. student with the opportunity to present evidence of his art and skill in teaching at the community-junior college, in addition to demonstrating his grasp of the scholarship, research techniques, and high degree of professionalism expected of the community-junior college teacher. The oral examination will probe for broad, in-depth, introspective teaching.

Both the improved traditional degree and new degree programs for faculty stress an experiential as well as cognitive education about the community-junior college. They are both teaching-oriented revisions of research-oriented graduate programs. On these program emphases, all sides seem to agree.

A poll of community-junior college administrators within the Southern Association of Colleges and Schools was taken in 1969 to determine if they felt the doctor of arts in teaching degree would satisfy the academic needs of the junior college. Most respondents had a favorable opinion toward the proposed doctor of arts in teaching degree and felt it would generally be accepted by junior college instructors, but they did not favor a research-oriented dissertation as part of the degree. These administrators substantially agree on the desirability of an advanced degree designed especially for community-junior college instructors [Shell, 1969].

A more recent survey was made in November, 1971, by the Professional Development Committee of the Illinois Association of Community and Junior Colleges Faculty Division. The committee surveyed both administrators and instructors regarding continued education of faculty for the purpose of providing guidance to the many universities who would be developing programs designed for the community-junior college instructor.

From this survey, this committee concludes that:

there seems to be a strong indication that both administrators and faculty members are interested in faculty continuing their education for credit. They are definitely subject matter oriented, generally frown on foreign language requirements, place little if any faith in the appropriateness of entrance examinations such as the Miller Analogy and Graduate Record Examinations, and lean to drastically reduced residency requirements. Faculty members placed more emphasis on the appropriateness of research than did their administrators, but neither placed much emphasis on primary research. Administrators seem to feel that the Doctor of Arts is the most appropriate degree for their faculty to work toward while faculty members in many cases, perhaps not knowing what the Doctor of Arts was, rated the Ph.D. as a slightly more desirable degree. [Rezner, 1971.]

The debate about the program name continues unresolved. However, an agreement about program content and goals over-shadows that debate. Eventually this agreement will turn new graduate programs toward meeting the true needs of community-junior college faculty. However, at present, the reader should remember that most community-junior college faculty-preparation programs are non-existent. Most prospective faculty do not, apparently, attend the few limited programs for specific community-junior college preservice education, much less the improved experiential programs. Thus, while there is a corner to be turned in this form of education, most programs have not reached that corner yet.

Vocational-Technical Educator Programs

The preceding programs have primarily considered the needs of academic subject teachers in community-junior colleges; very little attention has been paid to the preparation of teachers of technical-vocational subjects. Today, most of these teachers are asked to present a master's degree to the community-junior college. However, appropriate work and school experiences below the master's level are still a welcome substitute at many institutions.

A Work-Study Conference of experienced vocational-technical instructors [Feirer, 1970] characterized this instructor as an imparter of skills and knowledge, a creator of favorable learning environments, a counselor of youth and/or adults, a contributor to curricular change, a coordinator who works with industry, and a placement officer who places and follows up his graduates and dropouts. This multi-talented individual must receive appropriate preservice education for his duties at the community-junior college. The Illinois State Board Committee on community-junior college teacher preparation [1969] believes that university programs may be desirable but not necessary for this education. The traditional degree models applied to technical teachers may be misleading and, in some instances, completely inappropriate. For this reason, the Committee encourages community-junior colleges to develop standards of competence other than degrees for the recognition of technical teachers.

At the same time, the Committee encourages universities to develop degree programs at both the baccalaureate and advanced-degree levels to meet the need for technical teachers. In any case, the teacher of occupational education should be recognized on the basis of his competence rather than on degrees he may or may not possess.

Improvements upon vocational teacher education programs often center around the prospective or present community-junior college vocational student. The previously mentioned workshop of occupational education instructors recommends two such programs: Partnership and Pyramid. The Partnership Program would be for students who indicate a desire to become teachers before they enter the community-junior college as students. They would go through a pre-industrial teaching program somewhat similar to the current "transfer program," followed by attendance at a senior institution where they would take general and professional education courses and possibly participate in a co-op program.

The other program, the Pyramid Program, would be designed for students who decide to become teachers after entering or graduating from the community-junior college. This program would expect the senior institution to tailor a teacher education program which fits the needs of these students who have completed regular vocational-technical programs at the community-junior college [Feirer, 1970].

The Union for Research and Experimentation in Higher Education received a $62,000 USOE grant in 1971 to develop plans for preparation of two-year college teachers. Selected colleges would offer a four-year program leading to bachelor's and master's degrees. Students would enter the program after completion of two years of college. Their next three years would combine course work with appropriately spaced extra-academic experience so students would gain first-hand acquaintance with industrial, professional, social, and educational aspects of society. The fourth year would include a two-thirds time internship in residence at a junior college and one-third time master's project. For prospective two-year college teachers of occupational subjects who already have occupational knowledge and experience, a one-year combination study and internship program is proposed.

In July , 1971, Washington Technical Institute submitted a group of proposals in cooperation with the American Association of Junior College's Joint Committee Staff Development. One of the proposals concerned the development of a preservice master's degree model to prepare experienced occupational education graduates of community-junior colleges for community-junior college teaching.

The hypothesis of this proposal is that individuals who have graduated from a community-junior college and who have a minimum of two-years work experience in their special field have been overlooked as potentially fine teacher candidates for community-junior college. If this is in fact the case, it should be possible to design — with planning assistance and involvement of such candidates — a curriculum model which would capitalize on their experience and motivation.

It is proposed that through an intensive week-long workshop followed by three one-day writing sessions, a unique curriculum model be developed leading to the B.S. and TM.S. degrees in ten academic quarters. Phase II of such a proposal would include a request for funds to provide extensive scholarship monies whereby a selected group of community-junior college graduates in technical fields with at least two years of work experience could participate in the educational program for a maximum of ten quarters.

In these suggested vocational educator preservice programs, the emphasis on internship experience is applied in two ways. First, the potential educator would be experienced with the community-junior college, but as a two-year college student as well as teacher of these students. Second, the potential educator would be experienced as a worker in his field as well as teacher of his field. These proposed programs join the major and improved preservice programs for administrators and academic subject faculty in their emphasis on the internship.

Professional Services Staff

Professional services staff are usually considered to be student personnel workers and librarians. However, new cadres of specialists and paraprofessionals are becoming vital members of the staff at many community-junior colleges. This section includes discussion of the preparation of these new services staff members as well as the preparation of traditional staff.

Again, the EPDA has funded fellowship programs and institutes which may have a vital role in the preservice preparation of these staff members. For 1971–72, the EPDA granted money for eight programs with seventy-five fellowships for educational specialists, one program with eight fellowships for educational specialists and administrators, and eleven with 151 fellowships for educational specialists and teachers. Most of these programs for specialists were for student personnel workers — especially counselors.

A model EPDA Institute was held during 1970–71 at California State College, Los Angeles, for community-junior college student personnel counselors and administrators. The objectives of the program were to assist each enrollee to:

(1) increase his understanding of the function of the community-junior college and technical institute as parts of the social institution of education,

(2) contribute to his knowledge of the role of the two-year college in urban society serving the disadvantaged population,

(3) contribute to his knowledge of the dynamics of human behavior with special attention given to the implication of individual differences,

(4) gain a knowledge of the occupational structure of our society with its complexities and rapidly changing shape, form and content,

(5) develop increased skill in the use of tests and other appraisal techniques,

(6) develop competence in the utilization of theories and techniques of counseling through practicum experiences,

(7) improve knowledge of group process theory and practice,

(8) apply classroom learning through student personnel field work in local junior colleges, and

(9) participate with experienced junior college student personnel workers in focusing upon areas of major concern.

One of the programs for the new specialists is the sixth-year media degree offered by Eastern Illinois University. This program is designed to produce educators who can take leadership positions in community-junior colleges. The curriculum is designed to provide the skills and knowledge necessary for the media specialist to serve as a catalyst in bringing the benefits of modern technology into the teaching-learning situation. The program's core of courses is: Introduction to Audio-Visual Education, Preparation and Use of Instructional Materials, Television in Education, Audio-Visual Systems, Photography in Audio-Visual Education, Organization and Supervision of Audio- Visual Programs, Advanced Media Design, Communication Through Media, Field Experiences in Audio-Visual Education, Advanced Production and Photography, and Program and Script Writing for Education Television.

A paraprofessional is a person who can perform a significant role in a specialized area even though his education and training do not qualify him for full membership in a profession. Any discussion of the paraprofessional must deal with the source of his education. In the past, the education of the paraprofessional has been undertaken by many agencies. Although this is still true, two-year colleges have risen to prominence in this area and have provided preservice and inservice training for students as paraprofessionals. Although paraprofessionals have been used in a number of disciplines, i.e., English, math, foreign languages, their greatest development has been in the area of student personnel services.

Collins [1970] reports that paraprofessional counselor aides should receive a two-year A.A. degree education which consists of a core curriculum (behavioral science major with subject matter of the overriding societal issues of the day; ecology, racial conflict, etc.; math and elementary statistics; communication skills; interdisciplinary investigation of life styles, values, etc.) and specialized preparation in group test administration, scoring, and rough interpretation; interviewing techniques; collection and analysis of occupational information; referral and follow-up procedures, etc. The program should also include an internship.

This degree program's main goal would be the education of aides to assist counselors with walk-in clients, tests, occupational and education information, etc. Second, it would provide a people-oriented curriculum in the community college which would fill a need in the society and provide an open-ended career for those entering it. Third, it would enable minority group students to assist their peers and to help direct the college towards this assistance. Finally, it might become the model for preparation of professional counselors, with the internship extended through junior, senior, and graduate years.

At Harrisburg Area Community College, students are selected and trained to function as counselors as an aid to incoming students, particularly minority students [Pyle, 1971]. An effort is made to select students who exhibited a sincere regard for others, ability to accept different value systems, a capacity for empathy, and a healthy regard for self, plus the dimensions of autonomy, affiliation, intraception, dominance, and aggression on the Edwards Personal Preference schedule. The training program centers around core conditions of understanding, regard, and genuineness. The acquisition of interpersonal skills and the development of personal attitudes are the objectives of the training program. Through various experiences (role playing, small encounter groups) the selected students are exposed to behaviors which promote and diminish the helping relationship.

Most student counselors report four to six contacts with counselees per week, consisting mainly of providing support during crises associated with initial contact with the college environment and the suddenly increased expectations for one's own behavior and personality responsibilities. Student counselors appear most effective in helping students translate this tension into a positive effort which builds individual values. Two distinct groups request assistance: those concerned with acquiring information necessary to adapt to college environment and those concerned with long-range objectives, i.e., self-goals, curriculum selection, and vocational decision-making. Both groups have benefited from the psychological suport and practical assistance provided by student counselors.

Ware [1971] reports that Los Angeles City College has developed a Peer Counseling Program. The program at Los Angeles moves in these directions: (1) supervised training, (2) measurement of outcomes, (3) the delineation of objectives for the peer counselors, and (4) their use as facilitating agents for growth.

After two years of experimentation with peer counseling, Los Angeles City College has integrated the program into the instructional curriculum on a permanent basis, coordinating the activities of the faculty advisers and student counselors with the director of the Peer Counseling Program. He meets one hour per week with the peer counselors as part of their on-the-job training program designed to help peers enhance interpersonal relationships and to give them experiences in group dynamics. The program director also meets and confers with the faculty advisers regarding the structure of each weekly orientation and directs the involvement between faculty advisers and peer counselors in coordinated efforts to provide a continuously unique orientation, to the college life. Peer counselors work closely with professional counselors, who are often faculty advisers of orientation groups, to provide strong support for their counselees.

The program director is a member of the psychology department, as well as a member of the counseling staff. This combination puts him in a position to demonstrate the feasibility of giving college credit to the peer counselors on the bases of their inservice instruction as well as the interaction with the counselees.

The proposals of the Washington Technical Institute and the American Association of Junior Colleges extended beyond the realm of vocational-educator preservice preparation. At least two proposals were made for the preservice development of paraprofessional aides.

One proposal was made to develop and test a career-ladder teacher-aide development program which might also lead students to full professional status as community-junior college teachers with master's degrees.

The career ladder would give prospective teachers an opportunity to become involved in early teacher experiences. The program would enable low-income minority students to earn and learn their way to becoming fully qualified teachers.

Teachers in feeder high schools would identify students who could be encouraged to enroll in the local community college. The students would take an innovative program which would combine teacher aide experiences, professional teacher education courses, general education, and education experiences in an academic speciality. The student would accept more responsibility and receive increases in salary as he progressed through the program. This method would provide motivation, direct application of learning, and a means for the low-income minority student to pay his college expenses. Upon receiving the associated degree, the student would transfer to the appropriate university with full credit, and would use the same approach until he could assume the duties and responsibilities of the classroom teacher in the community-junior college. After completing the B.A. degree and during the M.A. program, the process would be continued with nearly full-time involvement in teaching activities as a qualified teacher at the community-junior college level.

Another proposal would provide preservice development experiences for future leaders and advisers of occupational youth organizations. The purpose of the proposal is to demonstrate the value of occupational youth organizations as a leadership tool and to develop a program which would train professional personnel to guide these occupational youth organizations in the high schools and community-junior colleges of the nation.

Low-income minority students often found in occupational education curriculums and other high-potential low achievers need new options where they can develop and put to work leadership skills and expertise in their own peer group relationships. The occupational youth organization structure is a natural vehicle for the development of such skills.

The students could continue their education and work simultaneously on a high school diploma and an associate degree as a teacher associate or in an occupational youth group leadership associate. The students could be paid wages out of work-study money, or the operational and student allowance expenses might be supported as a Manpower Development Training program.

2. INSERVICE PROGRAMS
Administrators

In 1959, the AAJC's Commission on Administration made recommendations concerning the types of inservice development programs which would be appropriate for community-junior college administrators. These recommendations were designed to aid universities with Kellogg Foundation grants in preparing relevant inservice programs for practicing administrators. Included in the recommendations were:

(1) The development of programs for newly appointed administrators as well as for those already experienced in the field;

(2) the provision of consulting services to community colleges;

(3) the establishment of seminars and workshops covering a wide range of topics of interest to practicing administrators;

(4) the development of programs for deans, governing board members and other administrative staff as well as presidents;

(5) the development of refresher programs for practicing administrators to provide an ongoing development experience. [Giles, 1961.]

During the 1960s, the Commission's recommendations were implemented in one form or another by participating universities across the country. Inservice development of community college administrators was not limited solely to Kellog-supported universities. Other academic institutions and the AAJC itself initiated numerous programs designed to aid administrators in performing their tasks more effectively.

Perhaps the most prominent forms of inservice education today are professional conferences and college or university seminars, workshops and institutes. Also available are internships, post-doctoral study opportunities, and the professional research publications for community-junior college staff.

Conferences

Typically, conferences are organized on a regional or national basis, revolve around a specific theme of current importance such as Institutional Research in Junior Colleges or The Junior College President, and are sponsored jointly by universities, junior college groups, and by governmental agencies such as the U.S. Office of Education. Johnson's [1971] example of a national conference which typically attracts community college administrators is that conducted by the University of California at Los Angeles Junior College Leadership Program in cooperation with the American Association of Junior Colleges, The League for Innovation in the Community College, and the National Laboratory for Higher Education. The theme of the 1971 National Conference featured the role and responsibilities of a newly emerging administrator, the educational development officer.

Perhaps of even more value to practicing administrators are local and regional conferences where the number of participants is considerably smaller, give-and-take participation easier, and the topics more specific. The annual Southern California Deans of Instruction Conference is a good example of such a regional gathering.

Seminars, Workshops and Institutions

More formal learning is available to administrators in the form of seminars, workshops and institutes. Such inservice education is available on an almost continuous basis throughout the year, with special emphasis given to the summer period. Programs of this type may last anywhere from one day to one year. The shorter seminar programs, usually several days in length, concentrate on specific topics such as Planning Programming and Budgeting Systems in Community Colleges, Designing the Community College Learning Resources Center, or Curriculum Decisions in Occupational Education [Giles, 1968]. In the case of the longer workshop and institute programs, the broad spectrum of community college administration may be addressed. For example, the Junior College Leadership Workshop is offered on a regular basis by several universities throughout the country. This workshop focuses upon such topics as:

(1) alternative models for decision-making;

(2) allocation of financial resources;

(3) role of state and local governing boards;

(4) faculty-administrator relations;

(5) recognition and accreditation;

(6) foundation and federal government support;

(7) staffing and personnel policies;

(8) student personnel services;

(9) programs for academically and economically disadvantaged students;

(10) institutional research;

(11) planning educational programs and faculties; and

(12) current research studies. [University of Illinois, 1968.]

Instructional staff for such programs are primarily drawn from the universities. The programs are usually held on university campuses. The content and structure of such workshops are typically determined by university faculty members in cooperation with advisory committees composed of experienced junior college administrators. Admission to these programs is usually open to any practicing, and in some cases, prospective, community-junior college administrator.

In the last several years, emphasis has been placed upon training newly-appointed administrative personnel separately from their more experienced colleagues. A concurrent emphasis upon dedicating workshops to only one type of administrator, such as a president, dean of instruction, or dean of students has resulted in a number of new inservice offerings specializing in, for example, the newly-appointed community college president.

The Education Profession Developments Act has played a significant role in the establishment of these short-range educational experiences for administrators and other staff. In 1971–72, the EPDA has funded three types of experiences which attend to inservice needs, primarily:

(1) Institutes — community-junior colleges receive 82 per cent of the monies ($2,742,995) for 56 institutes to train 4102 participants.

(2) Short-Term — community-junior colleges receive 77 per cent of the monies ($215,486) for 9 short-term programs to train 578 participants.

(3) Special Projects — community-junior colleges receive 100 per cent of the monies ($1,413,146) for 17 special projects to train 1441 participants.

Short-term training programs are generally intensive full-time programs of less than four weeks' duration. Special projects and institutes may vary from six weeks to a year of either part-time or full-time study. Special projects include a variety of approaches for advanced study and, therefore, have no specific requirements applicable to all projects.

During the academic year 1970–71, California State College conducted three EPDA short-term (three weeks) education programs. These programs were designed for experienced student personnel administrators from community-junior colleges and technical institutes; they concerned designated problem areas. It was felt that by concentrating on specific topics, enrollees could clarify issues, examine new materials and methods, and compare alternative choices and solutions. The three programs concentrated on:

(1) Preparing the paraprofessional for student personnel roles. Special emphasis was placed on preparing community leaders, culminating in career opportunities in student affairs.

(2) The much neglected area of placement and financial aid administration within the junior college. The topics discussed were job placement as a financial aid, on-the-job training, and terminal student placement programs. In the financial aid section, federal programs were discussed as was early commitments to the disadvantaged.

(3) The organization of student personnel programs in developing junior colleges. The outreach functions of the junior college to the greater community and the need to increase educational opportunity within the urban environment were emphasized.

Internships

Another form of inservice development is the internship. Although primarily used for preservice development efforts, some institutions have had considerable success with its use for experienced administrators as well. Some inservice internships are undertaken by those administrators who have had little preservice training; these internships may be part of a graduate program not unlike that taken by a preservice trainee. Other inservice internships may be used to expose practicing administrators to the functions, operations, and programs of state and federal government agencies with which they may have to deal on behalf of their college.

North Carolina State University's internship program is designed for both preservice and inservice education. The internship objectives are to:

(1) increase appreciation for the comprehensive community-junior college concept and the administrative processes of the community-junior college system;

(2) increase knowledge in the major areas of community college administration and appreciation of the relationships between them;

(3) develop proficiency in the use of behavioral science theory in identifying, analyzing and coping with administrative problems; and

(4) increase proficiency in community analysis, program planning, curriculum development, and program administration in the community college system. [Adams, 1967.]

Some inservice internships have been developed to familiarize the administrator with government agencies with which he has to deal. The AAJC has initiated a program which is designed to strengthen community-junior college administration through familiarizing participating administrators with those processes and programs of specific government agencies which relate directly to community-junior colleges.

A candidate for selection must have some responsibility for dealing with federal and state educational assistance programs in his college. The internship is twelve weeks in length with the first six weeks oriented towards studying government processes, meeting government officials, and becoming thoroughly familiar with federal education programs at the AAJC office in Washington, D.C. For the next four weeks, the intern works in the office of one of his congressmen or senators, to acquaint himself with the legislative process. Finally, each intern spends two weeks in an appropriate federal regional office where he becomes familiar with the operation of the Office of Education and other related agencies. The AAJC program has been funded by the U.S. Office of Education and has attempted to draw interns from throughout the country [Olson, 1971].

Post-Doctoral Study

Another form of inservice training which has received emphasis in recent years is the post-doctoral program. Typically, a fellowship is made available to the post-doctoral student. His activities may include teaching and participating in seminars and advanced courses in community college administration, working with interns in community college administration, as well as participating in field studies and research efforts carried on by the host institution. Upon completion of his post-doctoral studies, the fellow may take a position with a community college or may join another university or college with the intent of specializing in the community-junior college field [Johnson, 1971].

Research Publication

Additional inservice education for community college administrators and other staff hopefully results from the considerable amount of published research on community colleges. Through professional journals such as the *Junior College Journal,* the Educational Resources Information Clearing House (ERIC), and special publications produced by the universities, the government, and the American Association of Junior Colleges, administrators are given inservice opportunities to keep up with problems and practices of current interest in the community-junior college field.

Faculty

In 1969 and 1970, the American Association of Junior Colleges made two major attempts to assess the condition of faculty and other staff inservice education programs in community-junior colleges. The earlier attempt surveyed senior administrator opinions about faculty inservice programs. The latter was a national study of existent workshops and short courses for the professional improvement of community-junior college staff; this study was conducted by the AAJC Faculty Development Project with the cooperation of the Carnegie Corporation of New York.

The 1970 survey disclosed the following facts:

(1) There were 276 workshop and short course inservice programs conducted in 1970 for community-junior college staff.

(2) Thirty-seven percent were in academic areas. (Thirty-one percent of these were offered under the National Science Foundation.)

(3) Ten percent were in vocational-technical areas.

(4) Thirty-three percent were in education, curriculum development and learning theories.

(5) Thirteen percent were offered in administration and management.

(6) Seven percent were offered in student services area.

(7) One percent were offered in miscellaneous areas, i.e., one program in Europe.

Workshops and short courses are not the only inservice education experiences for staff, of course. However, the total of 276 such programs is virtually infinitesimal in comparison with the needs of about 130,000 staff members at over 1000 community-junior colleges [AAJC, 1971].

The survey revealed also that sixty percent of the inservice programs were held in two major geographical regions: the North Central (Illinois,

Indiana, Iowa, Kansas, Michigan, Minnesota, Missouri, Nebraska, North Dakota, Ohio, South Dakota, Wisconsin) and Western (Alaska, Arizona, California, Colorado, Hawaii, Idaho, Montana, Nevada, New Mexico, Oregon, Utah, Washington, and Wyoming). No vocational-technical inservice programs were reported in the Southern Region (Alabama, Arkansas, Kentucky, Louisiana, Mississippi, Oklahoma, Tennessee and Texas). Thus, these inservice programs are concentrated in two geographic areas where community-junior colleges are best established. While this location of programs follows a form of logical placement, it also means that the "rich get richer" while many "poorer" college staff members do not get the inservice education which is necessary for the welfare of their students and their colleges.

The 1969 survey of administrators confirmed the generally dismal state of inservice programs for community-junior college faculty. Ninety-five percent of all (288) respondents "expressed their conviction that the training which their people needed was *not* adequately available within their regions at least at the present time" [AAJC, *In-Service,* 1969]. This response led the AAJC to comment that a "serious national 'training gap' [existed] . . . in every section of the country."

Table 4 shows the types of general training which the senior administrators thought would fill the "gap." Table 5 shows the top three training priorities within each type. The reader should note that a course on the "Philosophy, History and Goals of the Two-Year College" was the most requested specific educational experience for faculty members.

The administrator comments about the program availability could have been used as fairly accurate predictors of the results of the 1970 survey of workshops and courses:

According to the data collected, there seems to be only a handful of fields in which the training in greatest demand is available in significant quantity. Such a short list might include some National Science Foundation programs in the physical sciences; a number of courses in the philosophy, history and goals of the two-year colleges; and a few programs each on teaching techniques and methods, modern educational administration and general guidance and counseling.

APPENDIX E — TABLE 4

General Training Requested (Up to 3 Mentions per College)

Education, Curriculum and Learning	774
Academic	618
Vocational-Technical	549
Administration and Supervision	509
Aspects of the Two-Year College	495
Counseling and Guidance	398

APPENDIX E — TABLE 5

Specific Training Requested (Up to 3 Mentions per College)

Academic	
Remedial English	133
Remedial Reading	86
Afro-American Studies	77
Vocational-Technical	
Data Processing	114
Engineering-Related Programs	109
Para-Medical Programs	75
Education, Curriculum and Learning	
Programmed Instruction	118
Testing and Measurement	111
Learning Theory	110
Aspects of the Two-Year College	
Philosophy, History and Goals	160
Community Needs and Relations	122
Student Profile	86
Administration and Supervision	
Public Relations	118
Principles of Supervision	85
Business Management and Planning	66
Counseling and Guidance	
Group Dynamics	92
Minority Movements and Problems	87
Human Relations	76

Most of the administrators suggested directions for the method as well as the content of future inservice education programs. The following percentages reflect many of their opinions:

(1) 58.6 percent wanted the training to occur at the community college, while 28.5 percent thought that training programs should occur within fifty miles.

(2) 55 percent believed that the training should take place during the school year, whereas 28.3 percent wanted it during summer sessions, and 14.8 percent believed that it should be conducted during vacations and breaks.

(3) 30.5 percent felt that a training program should last between one and two weeks, while 29 percent thought that it should last less than one week, and 16.4 percent were in favor of two- to four-week sessions.

(4) 62 percent believed that credit for inservice training was desirable, while 24.4 percent felt that it was unnecessary.

(5) Regarding their own colleges, 53 percent stated that workshops and short courses were fairly available, whereas 41.9 percent said that they were unavailable.

(6) When asked if their colleges would pay for such training, 28.4 percent stated they would pay up to one-half of the cost; 26.4 percent said that none of the cost would be covered; 18.7 percent stated that they did not know; 13.7 percent said that the full cost would be met; and 12.7 percent stated that between one-half and full cost would be covered.

Types of Inservice Experiences

In general, faculty inservice programs are of the same shape and form as administrator programs. This statement is true for the innovative and the established programs — conferences; workshops, seminars and institutes; internships; professional publications — all of these are available to both faculty and administrators.

There are some exceptions, of course. And this section begins with two of those programs which are usually considered "for faculty members only," although one has traditionally involved administrators and the other has begun to attract administrators who are interested in its applicability to their role performance. These programs are, respectively, orientation and evaluation.

Orientation

Faculty orientation programs can be banal or meaningful, vital seminars or unintentional farces, parties with punch or wilderness retreats. The variety is endless. However, the orientation program — whatever its form or meaning — has long been considered an important, or perhaps the *only,* inservice experience for faculty at many colleges.

No one knows the precise number of orientation programs which are offered by American community-junior colleges. Probably the percentage of programs exceeds the 37 percent which Eaton [1964] discovered in Michigan community-junior colleges in an early study. Almost every college has some sort of gathering of new and old faculty, perhaps even a "routine one-day introduction of new teachers to the administrative rhetoric and clerical confusions of a particular institution" [Kelly and Connolly, 1970], which is labeled "orientation."

But this gathering or one-day program is not really an effective orienter of new faculty. In fact, it may actually be a dis-orienter of faculty to institutions [Richards, 1964]. In such cases, new faculty turn to more experienced faculty for help. As a result, experienced faculty are often listed as the most important factors in the orientation of new faculty to the community-junior college [Richards, 1964; Eaton, 1964].

To be truly effective inservice experiences, orientation programs should be longer [Siehr, 1963]. They should also go "beyond the trees" of local institutions [Kelly and Connolly, 1970] to the broader forests of community-junior college issues.

Kelly and Connolly [1970] have created a model, long-range faculty orientation program. The model has the following characteristics:

(1) Planning utilizes a comprehensive team of people who have a direct influence and day-to-day impact on the functioning of the new faculty member.

(2) The orientation program is viewed in the perspective of an overall professional development plan, spaced over the initial time period most critical to the new faculty member's career transition — the first year.

(3) Four basic goals are offered as worthy of imaginative and focused effort by the planning team and the program leadership.

> To develop new faculty members with a knowledge and appreciation of the history, philosophy, and goals of community colleges in general and their institution in particular.
>
> To enable the new faculty member to be a growing, professional teacher and to comprehend the variability of student's intellectual characteristics, background, and certain nonintellectual factors that, as research on junior college students indicates, can either enhance or negate their performance.
>
> To describe and demonstrate to the new faculty member the full range of his role responsibilities both in and outside of the classroom. To make the new faculty member and his family as comfortable as possible in their new environment.

(4) The program leadership is nonhierarchical.

(5) Evaluation is perceived as part of a process of further planning and improvement.

(6) Orientation is viewed as a process balanced between the need for local indoctrination and a socialization to the environment of the junior college.

Kelly and Connolly's model incorporates many of the characteristics which Pettibone [1969] considers essential. Pettibone argues strongly for a long-range orientation concept. It considers the inservice dimension of the induction process to be crucial. He recommends that inservice programs be planned by a committee of faculty, administrators, and students; that feedback mechanisms be built into the planning phase; that major responsibility for orientation be given to the committee (rather than to the dean); that orientation be viewed in relation to both short-term and long-range goals; that short group meetings be balanced by a variety of events; that new faculty be surveyed before the inservice so that the programs will reflect their backgrounds; and that the family and social-community aspects of new job transition be made more visible in inservice programs.

The EPDA has funded at least one new orientation project which has attempted to reach the goals of Kelly and Connolly. The project has gotten "beyond the trees" with a unique first step toward an integrated orientation-inservice education program.

By means of an EPDA special project, Delaware County Community College has developed an inservice orientation program which can be experienced by staff at any time during the year. The goal of this project is to enable all staff to initiate their experience with the community college more knowledgeably and responsibly, especially in connection with the college's commitment to the disadvantaged student.

DCCC has already begun the pilot phase of the project by conducting faculty orientation through the mode of programmed self-instruction packages. The Self-Instruction Package Topics include Delaware County, The Community College Concept, Introduction to DCCC, The Community College Faculty, The Community College Student, and Innovations of Instruction.

During the second phase of the project, the college intends to utilize and evaluate the inservice materials and appropriately expand their use with all new staff members regardless of their time of entry at the institution. During the third phase of the project, the college will involve personnel representing each of the instructional houses, the Instructional Resources Department, the Student Personnel Office, and the nonprofessional staff in the development of inservice self-instructional materials centering on particular institution problems.

Evaluation as Inservice Education

Tracy [1961] surveyed the type of information desired by new faculty as part of their inservice programs. He discovered that large groups wanted such basic data as the objectives of their department, the objectives and content of the courses they were going to teach, the goals of the college and problems in meeting them, and the types of students enrolled in the college.

Ten years later, Tracy's study fits in well with the emphasis of the community-junior college upon "accountability" and the delineation of instructional, curriculum and individual objectives. In recent years, evaluation — through objective approaches and audio-tutorial devices — has come to the fore as a means for faculty improvement and inservice development.

Schafer [1970] advanced the Planned Faculty Professionalization Technique (PFPT) as a technique to facilitate instructional improvement in junior college systems. In the PFPT, first, careful development of institutional objectives in faculty development must be achieved. System-wide planning should include a careful assessment of the facilities, physical and human, that are available. Secondly, planning must be carefully done so that the balance of the system will not be thrown toward entropy by the involvement of system components in this new technique, PFPT. Thirdly, assessment of individual growth objectives on the part of each faculty member is essential to the functioning of PFPT. The faculty member, working with his immediate supervisor and colleagues, should define for himself specific and concise behavioral objectives to help improve the quality of his instruction.

Each individual faculty member should then be provided with background materials that will help him to undertake those activities which will assist him in reaching his goals. A series of alternative means must be incorporated within the PFPT of the individual faculty member to reach his specific goals so that coordination between PFPT plans can be facilitated. Each alternative pathway to reaching individual growth objectives should also include estimates of the most likely date for completion, the earliest date for completion, and the latest date for completion of the pathway.

The specific objectives of each faculty member, the objectives' relationships to one another, and alternative pathways for reaching these objectives should be set forth in a standardized manner. The faculty member and his immediate supervisor should be in a position to prepare a PFPT form, which will be, in fact, the individual professional growth plan for the faculty member. Schafer [1970] provides guidelines for development of the Planned Faculty Professionalization Technique Form.

Cohen has proposed a program similar to Schafer's PFPT. As a model of instruction or an inservice procedure to improve instructional competency, Cohen suggests a four-person department to facilitate departmental team planning, development of measures of evaluation, selection and building of media, and motivation of instruction.

Cohen feels a properly-oriented program director, setting out to rebuild a program, recognizes the necessity of specifying outcomes, plotting learning sequences, and collecting evidence of student gain. He, consequently, arranges for appropriate help to achieve his instructional goals. Thoroughly grounded in his subject area, he determines concepts, principles, and data to be learned. He builds objectives in terms of student behaviors.

He selects one of his instructors who has demonstrated evaluative ability to build measures for student performance in and out of class. This specialist is concerned with how the educational program brings all students closer to the stated goals of the college.

The next team member is a media specialist, a person with full knowledge of books, programmed texts, films, film strips and recordings in the field. He has ability to construct appropriate materials as needed. The media specialist plots the learning paths.

The fourth member of the team is picked as a discussion leader, a motivator, an instructor with patience and skill to bring about student interaction.

In 1967, Salatino commented that "the hope of the junior college to improve instruction necessarily, lies in the in-service area." He then outlined an Auto-Student-Peer-Regional (ASPR) evaluation procedure for the inservice development of faculty in New England community-junior colleges. The ASPR inservice technique included four ingredients: (1) auto-critique self-evaluation method, (2) the student questionnaire, (3) peer evaluation, and (4) evaluation from a regional evaluating faculty group. The primary part of the process is teacher self-evaluation. The other three methods facilitate teacher improvement of instructional techniques.

Auto-critique evaluation is done primarily through the use of a video-tape recorder. This device provides the teacher with an opportunity to see himself in his teaching role. His strengths and weaknesses can be observed. Recommendations for improvement can be made.

Student evaluation should add some validity to faculty self-evaluation. Most observers feel students are perfectly capable of saying whether the teacher has made an organized, well-presented, informative presentation which has helped them to learn. This evaluation approach will tell the faculty member something about the impact that he has on his students.

Peer evaluation is a process whereby any college faculty member might be called to evaluate the effectiveness of another. Lastly, the use of regional faculty evaluators could give expert opinion regarding the individual's skill as a teacher; they could also present helpful suggestions and criticisms regarding an entire department's strengths and weaknesses.

Ohlone College has begun a Sequenced Peer Teaching (SPT) project for the improvement of instruction. For the SPT project, the following goals were set:

(1) Encouragement of faculty to use video-taping as part of classroom instruction.
(2) Encouragement of the use of in-class video-tapes for analysis of instruction.
(3) Development of a means for peer interaction for improvement of instruction.
(4) Development of skills and processes for the observation, description and analysis of instruction.
(5) Identification and reinforcement of effective instruction.
(6) Identification and modification of ineffective instruction.

Sequenced Peer Teaching brings colleagues together in small groups for mutal assistance in the development of teaching skills. Group members teach one another. The presentations are video-taped and played back for group critique. The assignments move in a sequence from brief, simpler initial presentation to longer, more complex presentations. The peer teaching takes place in a setting which is less complex than that of the classroom. Participants include faculty, administrators, and a facilitator from outside the college.

Other Forms of Inservice Education

Orientation and evaluation experiences are perhaps the oldest and newest forms of faculty inservice education opportunities in the community-junior college. The following opportunities — conferences; seminars, workshops and institutes; and internships — can also be valuable inservice experiences for faculty. Probably, conferences and seminars, workshops and institutes are the most popular available experiences.

Conferences

This section does not attempt to describe all the available conferences for faculty inservice education. Such description or even a simple listing might be impossible since every faculty member and every institution can belong to myriad professional associations which have conferences each year.

The educational value of conferences can vary according to the disposition of each participant. Some participants go to teach and learn; others go to find new jobs; still others go for the joy and informal education of socialization with professional colleagues.

The merits of conferences cannot be tallied neatly on reference cards. However, this section describes three conferences with potential merit for all who attend. The three conferences vary according to style of presentation and goals.

The Bennett Conference at Keystone Junior College has been meeting since 1963. The entire program comes from within the conference. The conferees consist of two-year college faculty from different disciplines, different geographical areas and varying experience in junior college teaching. The basic concept of this conference is to provide an opportunity for inservice training of master teachers.

The conference is as flexible and unstructured as possible. The philosophy of the conference is best expressed by a quote from its founder, Roger Garrison:

Our basic premise was both simple and an assertion of faith; that if you bring together people of good will and intelligence, who have aims in common; if you give them an informal situation, comfortable, free from pressure — either from superiors or from arbitary demands; and if you insist only that they speak their minds freely — and allow the freedom to others — trying to find common denominators of experience and insight; something good will come of it for each person.

The 1970 theme of the Bennett Conference was Interdisciplinary Instruction: A Discussion of Integration and/or Integrity in Two-Year Colleges. It was reported that the theme received considerable support from the fact that a number of the participants brought with them experience and preparation in interdisciplinary situations and systems approaches to instruction.

Educators participating in the 1970 Bennett Conference decided that concerted efforts should be made to set up small inservice training centers in various cities — specifically mentioned were New York, Chicago, San Francisco, Atlanta, Dallas, etc. — and, in a way, duplicate the Bennett situation on a year-round basis.

In August, 1970, the first inservice Division Chairman Leadership Conference was held at Orange Coast and Golden West Colleges located in Costa Mesa and Huntington Beach, California.

Thirty-three division chairmen representing 24 league colleges in nine states spent two weeks studying the emerging role of chairman for the 1970's. The task of the conference was to define better the role of the chairman, his interpersonal relationships, to become realistic about needed innovation and to compile a conference syllabus useful for division chairmen.

The Association for Education Communications Technology set up to sponsor a National Conference on Instruction Assessment, via a telenetwork. The Conference was booked simultaneously on three community-junior college campuses in 1972. It may provide a model for such conferences in the future. The three campuses are Burlington, Pemberton, N.J.; Moraine Valley Community College, Palos Hills, Illinois; and Tarrant County Junior College, Fort Worth, Texas. In each place a series of national programs were set up to be broadcast at all sites. Then a response by a prominent figure in the field of instructional development was to be carried live by a telephone network to all three colleges. Participants are able to question this response. Each campus was also to produce a local program to provide still more discussion and a local focus on the national program. The national presentations were aimed on innovative programs in developmental studies (mathematics, reading, English), use of media and physical education (such as swimming and tennis), and business education (use of continuous progress and multimedia methods).

Seminars, Workshops and Institutes

Seminar, Workshop and Institute programs for faculty follow the same general format as those for administrators. Thus, rather than being simply repetitious, this section describes several innovative attempts to make these programs more valuable inservice education experiences.

From the Bennett Conference concept, inservice training programs for master teachers have been developed in many parts of the nation.

An example of such inservice training is shown in the Great Teachers Seminars. Garrison [1969], reports that in August, 1969, sixty-nine community-junior college instructors lived and worked together for ten days at Westbrook Junior College (Maine) in the first seminar for great teachers. Their primary concerns were the improvement of instruction; development of fresh, effective teaching methods; and the communication of these ideas with fellow teachers across the nation. Considerable concern and speculation surrounded the fact that only one or two of the participants were vocational-technical instructors. There was concern that the selection process tended to focus inordinately on those from the more "traditional" college disciplines.

Washington Technical Institute and the American Association of Junior Colleges have developed two interesting proposals for inservice seminars. The first proposal is entitled, "A Proposal for Conducting Staff Development Seminars on Understanding the Awareness Role of Faculty, Staff, Administration, and Community (including Industry) in Serving the Low-Income Minority Youth in Emerging Institutions."

This proposal includes the planning and implementation of 20 seminars over a year-long period. The seminars would involve staff and policy makers such as board members, community and industrial leaders, and students in the training sessions.

The main purpose would be to collect needed information regarding the total potential student population to be served. The emphasis would be on low-income minority groups which are not served by the college at present. In addition, new emerging types of curriculum would be identified which would anticipate manpower needs and provide community service. A model would be developed in which inservice training programs would be geared to further broaden the awareness of the faculty, administration, and community leaders.

The second proposal, "A Proposal to Conduct a Series of Ten Workshops Involving One Hundred Experienced and Inexperienced Community College Personnel Using Their Collective Knowledge to Design a Number of Approaches for In-Service Staff Development Programs," appears quite promising. These seminars would be held at local community college campuses on an average of two per month. The groups would be comprised of experienced and inexperienced community-junior college personnel (faculty, administration, and students) in equal numbers. A number of different concerns and a variety of inservice models would be expected to emerge from the seminars.

At De Anza College, a Committee on Faculty Development has developed workshop programs to:

(1) help newly-employed faculty members to become fully-functioning members of the staff,

(2) help all faculty members to improve the quality of instruction,

(3) help all faculty members to stay abreast of the "knowledge explosion" in their fields as well as in the art and science of education,

(4) help all faculty members to grow personally and professionally, and

(5) help all faculty members to advance the purpose of De Anza College.

The committee has arranged for both a fall and a spring series of workshops covering a wide range of professional concerns: educational media, curriculum, ethnic studies, etc. But any college group may organize a workshop at any time providing approval is received from the committee. The college provides remuneration for consultants, facilitators, and course organizers. While the inservice workshops are designed for the purpose of assisting faculty, staff, and administrators in their continuing occupational development, credit earned may be used for advancement of the college salary schedule.

On a broader, intercollege basis, the Illinois Mathematics Workshop Program has been formed. The program consists of a sequence of two-day workshops attended by about fifty two-year college representatives from approximately twenty-nine colleges participating in this cooperative program. In addition to these fifty representatives, observers are invited from other two-year colleges or from four-year colleges. The first two of these workshops were held on the Urbana campus of the University of Illinois, while the remaining four have been held in central Illinois communities. The workshops have been held during the fall and spring of each of the three years of the program.

Each workshop has emphasized the professional development of the participants. The participants have been directly involved in the operation of the workshops by acting as group leaders, by serving on workshop writing teams, and by taking part in the planning of workshop agendas and activities.

Each workshop has developed a report describing specific recommendations from the participants for the improvement of two- and four-year college programs in mathematics.

The Danforth Foundation has developed a workshop which has been concerned with the area of improvement of undergraduate instruction since 1957. The central purpose of the Workshop is to provide an opportunity for intensive study and discussion of ways and means for improving the quality of liberal arts education at the undergraduate level. The Foundation believes that there are all too few opportunities in American higher education for faculty, students, and administrative officers to join in serious consideration and unhurried discussion of the large issues of educational policy — the issues which transcend a single discipline, a single institution, a single country.

The Danforth Foundation has also proposed a new Community College Institute. In August 1972, the Danforth Foundation proposes to bring together for a twelve- to fifteen-day conference at Stephens College, Columbia, Missouri, teams of six staff members from twenty community-junior colleges across the United States. Each team will include faculty members, students, administrators, and one trustee. The teams will attend various seminars led by national experts; they will work with these experts to design a project to improve some aspect of teaching on their campuses. Once a project is designed, the teams will return home to implement the project and return for a follow-up session at the community-junior college institute in April, 1973, for a period of five to seven days to review project development and consider further needs for development. Danforth will provide all expenses for the teams and funds for the development of some of the projects for which the individual colleges can apply.

De Nevi [1970] reports that the EPDA has funded an innovative Institute for Junior College Teachers of Disadvantaged Students from Urban Ghettos which has offered twenty white, middle-aged, middle-class teachers first-hand exposure to slum life. Instruction was conducted by hard-core ghetto youths from a San Francisco self-help organization. It consisted of tours of the ghetto community to take an active part in the average daily life of slum area students (afternoons). Instruction in the mornings was held in classrooms of the City College of San Francisco, where experts lectured on legal and medical problems of the poor, employment, community-action programs, and school decentralization. Initially, these community-junior college teachers had attitudes such as "I know, but what can I do?" These attitudes became more marked by understanding, willingness, and ability to teach. The teachers began to lose their ethnocentrism; they began to see how they might relate curriculum to the values of their students.

Perhaps the broadest inservice fellowship-institute program in the nation is being developed by a western consortium of community-junior colleges. The consortium includes the community-junior colleges of the Bay Area of California and of selected urban areas of Arizona, Colorado,

Hawaii, Oregon, and Washington. These colleges propose to work together in cooperation with the University of California, Berkeley, to establish and share staff development programs designed to improve student learning. Sharing staff development activities among the consortium of colleges could contribute to instructional innovation and improvement, conservation of scarce resources, improvement of evaluation, and creation of a model for study by other institutions interested in inter-campus programs for staff development. The proposal includes the request of funds for a program for twenty Professional Development Fellows. The fellowships will be distributed across the cooperating community colleges with the expectation that two of the fellows would serve with the staff of Programs in Community College Education at the University of California to help in planning and conducting consortium activities.

Among the aspects of the consortium program are:

(1) Faculty and administrators from the member colleges will be encouraged to observe programs at other colleges, and, by visitations and other modes of communication, to participate directly in innovative projects. This will be particularly true of the fellowship grantees who will be expected to serve as "learning fellows" as they identify fresh approaches to bring back to their own institutions, and as "teaching fellows" when transmitting successful developmental models to other members of the consortium. It is anticipated that a formal exchange program will accrue from these efforts to share problems and solutions across colleges.

(2) The combined fellowship-institute program will be continuous as it seeks to establish the general consortium structure, the identification of existing or new solutions to the problems of educating students in need, and in establishing procedures for sharing and transplanting successful programs within the consortium.

(3) The Professional Development Fellows and the consortium leadership will constitute the critical mass for the promotion of educational change across the consortium. In line with the best arguments for a non-traditional study, the fellows will serve as teacher-learners rather than pursue a tradition-bound program of graduate studies.

(4) The Professional Development Fellows will be selected jointly by the faculty of the cooperating community colleges and the program directors. Among the anticipated criteria for such selection will be past demonstration of innovative practices, interest in interinstitutional sharing, and evidence of potential as a change agent among peers. The instructors and assistant instructors will be similarly selected from the consortium colleges.

(5) The continuous institute concept includes a program of interchange workshops, exchange of television and audio cassettes, written and graphic progress reports of faculty development activities, and informal as well as formal visitations.

(6) With the conviction that the learning-teaching equation goes unrecognized in many pre and inservice programs, the proposed program will be devoted to reducing the artificial barriers between learning and teaching. Because of this commitment, the essential faculty for the combined fellowship and institute program will be supplemented by those faculty and administrators who are prepared to learn new ways of educating new students. Among the major roles of the directors and consultants will be the enhancement of this process of self-development.

Internships

A major part of the consortium program is the professional development fellows' visitations to other member colleges. Thus, the western consortium joins the many other groups and individuals who advocate internship experiences for faculty and administrator preservice and inservice education.

Professional Services Staff

In the preservice development section, an EPDA institute for those staff members was described. Such an institute might be described in this section also. In fact, this report has described many such preservice/inservice experiences which have been classified as either preservice or inservice. The reader is cautioned again about this multipurpose possibility of many programs which may seem to have only one educational purpose. In this report, the present emphasis rather than the possible use determines the classification of programs.

Once again, professional services staff utilize most of the forms of inservice education which are available to faculty and administrators. At least most full-professional staff do. The numbers of new specialists and paraprofessionals are so few and their emergence as staff is so recent that many of these inservice experiences are unavailable to them at present.

This section describes only one program — a comprehensive state-wide center approach to the inservice education of student personnel staff in New York State. The Two-Year College Student Development Center at the State University of New York has been in operation since 1968. Its goal is to promote total student development. One of its primary means to that goal is the development of personnel.

The Center's commitment to the preparation of personnel — both counselors and other student personnel workers — is designed to make these professional workers more qualified to carry out the responsibilities demanded by the two-year colleges and society. This function is accomplished largely through inservice education projects, workshops, demonstration projects and publications.

A major inservice education project was the development of group counseling models and experiences for vocational and other community-junior college counselors. The Center has also sponsored a series of workshops on vocational counseling for eighty-one participants from thirty-five colleges and urban centers in New York State. In 1970, an invitational seminar brought together national leaders and state personnel to discuss "Student Development in the Community College: Directions and Designs for the 70's." Other programs have been and will be offered as the Center attempts to move closer to its ultimate goal of total student development in the community-junior college.

In speaking for the Center, Robbins [1970] summarizes the need for inservice education — not only for student personnel and other specialist staff, but for all community-junior college personnel:

Social and educational changes require role changes with concomitant new learnings. Constant updating of pre-service graduate study is important. Sabbatical programs also are often a godsend to the harried professional who normally has little time to keep abreast with, let alone get ahead of recent developments in his field. However, it is only inservice education, both formal and informal, that can reach the regular teaching and staff faculty member at the time of his need. Primarily, it is in-service education — at least some phase of it — that can help the college in its attempt to revitalize and review itself.

Conclusions

In this section of the report, a variety of pre and inservice programs for community-junior staff are described. This is by no means an exhaustive survey. In the time limits of this report these programs were selected from available material to illustrate a number of existing and proposed approaches to staff development.

This very cursory survey reveals that there is no lack of imagination and creativity in program designs. But it is also clear that few of the designs have been implemented. Further, few of the implemented designs have been reviewed and evaluated.

If staff development programs are to be implemented, tested and evaluated, community-junior colleges must be provided funds so that such programs can become realities. Some of the programs described in this section of the report could serve as excellent models if funds become available.

References

Adams, Dewey A. "The Internship: An Innovative Approach to Providing Continuing Leadership for North Carolina's Community Colleges." *Adult Leadership,* Vol. 16, 1967, 218–232.

American Association of Junior Colleges. *AAJC Directory.* Washington, D.C.: 1971.

————. *Guide to In-Service Training for Two-Year College Faculty and Staff Members.* Washington, D.C.: 1970.

————. *In-Service Training for Faculty and Staff: A Survey of Junior and Community College Administrators.* (Faculty Development Project.) Washington, D.C.: 1969.

————. *Preparing Two-Year College Teachers for the '70's.* Washington, D.C.: 1969.

————. "Pre-Service Training of Two-Year College Instructors." *Junior College Journal,* Vol. 39, 1969, 7+.

Anderson, Duane D., et al. *Guidelines for the Preparation of Community-Junior College Teachers.* Washington, D.C.: National Faculty Association of Community and Junior Colleges, 1968.

Anderson, G. Lester. "Initiating Programs in Teaching, Administration and Research in Community Colleges." *Buffalo Studies: Administering the Junior College in a Changing World,* Vol. II, 1966. 183–190.

Besvinick, S. L. and Fryer, T. W. "Miami Begins the Diplomate in College Teaching." *Junior College Journal,* Vol. 37, 1969, 48+.

Blocker, Clyde E. "Are our Faculties Competent?" *Junior College Journal,* Vol. 36, 1965, 12–17.

Bossone, Richard M. *The Training and Work of California Public Junior College Teachers of English.* Riverside, California: Riverside County Superintendent of Schools, 1964.

Cardozier, V. R. "The Doctorate of Arts: A Review of the College Teaching Question." *Journal of Higher Education,* Vol. 37, 1968, 261–270.

Carnegie Commission on Higher Education. *A Digest of Reports and Recommendations, December 1968-October 1971.* Berkeley, California: 1971.

Carnegie Commission on Higher Education. *New Students and New Places: Policies for the Future Growth and Development of American Education.* New York: McGraw-Hill Book Company, 1971.

Case, Chester. "Cooperative Internship Program for Beginning Instructors in Community Colleges, 1970–71." Funded by the Department of Health, Education, and Welfare Title V-E, 90-35. University of California, Berkeley, California: 1970.

Cohen, Arthur M. *Developing Specialists in Learning.* Los Angeles: University of California, n.d.

————. "Teacher Preparation — Rationale and Practice." *Junior College Journal,* Vol. 37, 1967, 21–25.

————. *Focus on Learning: Preparing Teachers for the Two-Year College.* Occasional Report Number 11 from the UCLA Junior College Leadership Program. Los Angeles: 1968.

Cohen, Edward. "Faculty for Teaching-Learning: Proposed New Graduate Centers for Systematic Preparation of Community College Teachers." Report to the Union for Research and Experimentation in Higher Education. Yellow Springs, Ohio: 1970.

Collins, Charles C. "Giving the Counselor a Helping Hand." *Junior College Journal,* Vol. 40, 1970, 17–20.

Connolly, John J. "Will the Community College Survive the Ph.D. Surplus?" *Educational Record,* Summer, 1971, 272+.

DeNevi, D. "Retreading Teachers the Hard Way." *Junior College Journal,* April, 1970.

Dunham, E. A. "Rx for Higher Education: The Doctor of Arts Degree." *Journal of Higher Education,* Vol. 41, 1970, 505–515.

Eaton, John Mead. "A Study of Orientation of New Faculty Members in Michigan Community Colleges." Doctoral dissertation. East Lansing: Michigan State University, 1964.

Feirer, John L. and Lindbeck, John R. "Development of Junior-Community College Curricula for Future Teachers of Industrial Education: An Interim Report." Los Angeles: Educational Resources Information Clearinghouse, 1970.

Friedman, Norman L. "The Public Junior College Teacher in a Unified Public School System." Doctoral dissertation. Columbia: University of Missouri, 1965.

Garrison, Roger. *Junior College Faculty: Issues and Problems.* Washington, D.C.: American Association of Junior Colleges, 1967.

————. "1969 Seminar for Great Teachers." *Junior College Journal,* Vol. 40, 1969, 7–9.

————. "The Making of a College Teacher." Paper presented at the Twenty-Second National Conference on Higher Education, Chicago. The Association for Higher Education, March 6, 1967.

Giles, Frederic T. "Junior College Leadership Program." *Junior College Journal,* Vol. 31, 1961, 321–325.

————, and Schille, William J. "A Report on Activities: 1967–68, The Area of Higher Education. University of Washington Department of Education." Seattle, Washington: Center for the Development of Community College Education, 1968.

Gleazer, Edmund J. "Preparation of Junior College Instructors." *New Directions for Instruction in the Junior College,* ed., B. Lamar Johnson. Los Angeles, 1965, 25–29.

————. "Preparation of Junior College Teachers." *Educational Record,* Vol. 48, 1967, 147–152.

Hall, George L. "Clinical Training for Future Administrators." *Junior College Journal,* Vol. 34, 1963, 22–23.

Hedland, Dalva. "Preparation for Student Personnel: Implications of Humanistic Education." *Journal of College Student Personnel,* Vol. 12, 1971, 324–328.

Hill, C. R. and Tolle, D. J. *Making Teacher Education Relevant; Community College Internship Program.* Report to the Ford Foundation on the Five-Year Joint Project of the Junior College District of St. Louis — St. Louis County, Missouri and Southern Illinois University for Preparing Two-Year Post-High School Teachers. Carbondale, Illinois: 1971.

Howell, John M. "A Brief Against the Doctor of Arts Degree." *Journal of Higher Education,* Vol. 42, 1971, 392–399.

Idaho State University, "Graduate School Catalog." Bulletin of the Idaho State University, Vol. 25, No. 3. Pocatello, Idaho: 1971.

Illinois, University of, College of Education, Junior College Leadership Workshop. "A Summer Workshop for Prospective Junior College Administrators in Comprehensive Junior Colleges." Brochure. Urbana: 1968.

Institutes for New College Presidents. Brochure. University of California, Berkeley; Teachers College, Columbia University; University of Illinois; 1968.

Johnson, B. Lamar. (ed.) *The Improvement of Junior College Instruction.* Occasional Report Number 15 of a conference sponsored by the UCLA Junior College Leadership Program, the American Association of Junior Colleges, and the University of California Office of Relations with Schools. Los Angeles: 1969.

————. "Review of the Two-Year College." *Journal of Higher Education,* Vol. 35, 1964, 51–53.

————, and Kintzer, Frederick C. "How Internships Work." *Junior College Journal,* Vol. 33, 1963, 17–19.

————. "UCLA Junior College Leadership Program: A New Decade." A report prepared by the Graduate School of Education, University of California. Los Angeles: UCLA, 1971.

W. K. Kellogg Foundation. *Annual Report for 1961.* Battle Creek, Michigan: 1961.

————. *Toward Improved School Administration.* Battle Creek, Michigan: 1961.

Kelly, M. Frances. "Format Description and Evaluation: An Orientation Model." *Professional Development Project for Two-Year College Vocational and Technical Faculty.* Buffalo: State University of New York, 1968.

————, and Connolly, John J. *Orientation for Faculty in Junior Colleges.* Monograph No. 10. Washington, D.C.: American Association of Junior Colleges, 1970.

Koenker, Robert A. "Status of Doctor of Arts and Sixth-Year Degree and Non-Degree Programs for Preparing Junior College and College Teachers." Unpublished Paper. Cited in John J. Connolly, "Will the Community College Survive the Ph.D. Surplus?" *Educational Record,* Vol. 52, 1971, 268–270.

Larson, Howard A. "Preparation of Teachers for Two-Year Post Secondary School Programs." *Business Education Forum,* Vol. 25, 1970, 28–29.

Lusken, Bernard J. *A Workshop of Interest to New Presidents with Little Background in the Junior College: An Analysis.* Los Angeles: Educational Resources Information Center, 1967.

Matson, Jane. "Student Personnel Services in Two-Year Colleges." *Peabody Journal of Education,* Vol. 48, 1971, 276–281.

Mayhew, Lewis B. *Graduate and Professional Education, 1980: A Survey of Institutional Plans.* New York: McGraw-Hill Book Company, 1970.

McCuen, John T. "An Intern Reacts." *Junior College Journal,* Vol. 35, 1965, 24–26.

Medsker, Leland L. "Junior College Leadership Training Programs." *Journal of Secondary Education,* Vol. 36, 1961, 30–32.

Morgan, Don A. *Implications for the Junior College Leadership Training Program Drawn from a Continuing Study of the Two-Year College President.* Los Angeles: Educational Resources Information Clearinghouse, 1968.

Morrison, James Louis. "The Relationship of Socialization Experience, Role Orientation, and the Acceptance of the Comprehensive Community-Junior College Faculty." Doctoral dissertation. Tallahassee: Florida State University, 1969.

O'Banion, Terry. "A Core Program Proposal for the Preparation of College and University Student Personnel Workers." Doctoral dissertation. Florida State University, 1966.

Olson, Claire. "Governmental Interns." *Junior College Journal,* Vol. 41, 1971, 5.

Peterson, Basil H. *Critical Problems and Needs of California's Junior Colleges.* Modesto, California: California Junior College Association, 1965.

Pettibone, John F. "Orientation Programs and Orientation Leadership in the Public Two-Year Institutions of New York State." Doctoral dissertation. Columbus: Ohio State University, 1969.

Phair, Tom S. *A Profile of New Faculty in California Community Colleges.* University of California, Field Service Center, 1968.

Pyle, Robert P. and Snyder, Fred A., "Students are Para-professional Counselors at Community Colleges." *Journal of College Student Personnel,* Vol. 12, 1971, 259–262.

Rezner, C. Thomas. "Continued Education and the Junior College Professor." Dixon, Illinois: 1971. A Mimeograph Paper prepared for the Illinois Association of Community and Junior Colleges.

Richards, Jerrel Thurston. "Critical Incidents in the Orientation of Newly Appointed Junior College Instructors." Doctoral dissertation. Los Angeles: University of California, 1964.

Robbins, William A. *Report for the Year 1969–1970: Two-Year College Student Development Center.* A report prepared by the Two-Year College Student Development Center of the State Univrsity of New York. Albany: 1970.

Rouche, John and Boggs, John. "The Educational Development Officer Catalyst for Change." A paper prepared for the Regional Educational Laboratory for the Carolinas and Virginia. Durham, North Carolina: 1970.

Salatino, A. (ed.) *Teaching in the Junior College.* Providence, Rhode Island: Roger Williams Junior College, 1967.

Schafer, Michael I. "The Student Role of Teachers: Faculty Development in the Community College." A paper prepared for the Institute of Higher Education, University of Florida. Gainesville, Florida: 1970.

Schultz, Raymond E. "The Junior College President: Who and Where From." *The Junior College President,* ed., B. Lamar Johnson. Occasional Report Number 13 from the UCLA Junior College Leadership Program. Los Angeles: 1969, 7–17.

————, and Wattenbarger, James L. "A New Leadership Program for State Level Community-Junior College Professional Staff." *Junior College Journal,* Vol. 39, 1968, 26–27.

Shell, Edwin Taylor. "An Investigation of the Doctor of Arts Degree for the Junior College Instructor." A Report to the Southern Association of Colleges and Schools. Atlanta: 1969.

Siehr, Hugo E. et al. *Problems of New Faculty Members in Community Colleges.* East Lansing: Michigan State University, 1963.

Smolich, R. "The Status of Professional Education Courses/Programs Specific to the Two-Year College in 82 Schools of Education, 1969–1970." Mimeographed Survey. 1971.

Spencer, David K., "A Mini-Proposal Prepared by Mount Hood Community College for Participation as a Cooperating Institution in the AAJC/Washington Technical Institute Community College Teacher Education Proposal to the U.S. Office of Education." Unpublished. Gresham, Oregon: 1971.

St. Louis Junior College District. "Teaching Internships — Core Program. St. Louis, Missouri," n.d.

State of Illinois. *Report of the Illinois State Board of Higher Education Committee on the Preparation of Junior College Teachers: Master Plan Phase III.* Springfield: 1969.

Stratton, Alan G. "Needed: The Doctorate of Arts in College Teaching." *Junior College Journal,* Vol. 39, 1969, 19–23.

Stripling, Robert Olin. "The Orientation of the New College Faculty Member." Doctoral dissertation. New York City: Columbia University, Teachers College, 1964.

Strothman, F. S. *The Graduate School Today and Tomorrow.* On behalf of the Committee of Fifteen. New York: Fund for the Advancement of Education, 1955.

Texas Tech University. "An Institute for Pre-Service Training of Junior College Teachers." Lubbock: 1970.

Tracy, Norbert. "Orientation of New Faculty Members in Colleges and Universities." *North Central Association Quarterly,* Fall 1961, 214–221.

UCLA Junior College Leadership Program. "A New Decade." Los Angeles: Graduate School of Education, University of California, 1971.

University of Arizona, Department of English. "Proposal for the M.A. in English with Emphasis on Teaching in the Junior College." Unpublished. Tucson: 1969.

Ware, Claude. "The Los Angeles City College Peer Counseling Program." A Report sponsored by the U.S. Office of Equal Opportunity with cooperation of the American Association of Junior Colleges. Los Angeles: 1971.

Williams, Cratis. *A Master's Degree Program for Junior College Teachers.* A paper presented at the sixth annual meeting of the Council of Graduate Schools in the United States. Denver, Colorado: 1966.

Wortham, Mary. "The Case for a Doctor of Arts Degree: A View from a Junior College Faculty." *AAUP Bulletin,* No. 53. Washington, D.C.: 1967.

Yuhl, Walter A. *A Proposal for In-Service Training of Part-Time Evening Division Faculty.* A seminar paper prepared for the School of Education, University of California. Los Angeles, California: 1967.

Zane, Lawrence F. H. "The Demand for Community College Teachers and the EPDA Program Under the College of Education." Los Angeles: Educational Resources Information Clearinghouse. 1969.

Index

H

Harper, William Rainey, 3, 5
Harrisburg Area Community College
(Penna.), 151
Hawaii, University of, 138
Health occupations staff, 96
Heterogeneity of students, 37–39
Historical development of community-
junior college, 2–9
need for knowledge of by staff, 86
"Human development facilitator," 24
Human development specialists, 95;
see also Student personnel work
Humanistic teachers, 64–65, 87
Huther, John W., 13, 15

I

Illinois Mathematics Workshop
Program, 169
Illinois, University of, 129–30
Inhouse continuing seminars, 109
Innovation, 25–26
Inservice training programs, 1, 23, 58,
84–85, 101–12, 115–18, 153–73
Florida plan for, 105–106
for administrators, 153–58
for faculty, 158–72
for professional services staff, 172–73
state support for, 104–106
types of, 106–12
Institutes, 107–108, 153–56, 167–72
Instructional technology specialists, 96
Interdisciplinary education, 71–73
Internships, 86–87, 126–27, 130–32,
139–40, 156–57

J

Johnson, B. Lamar, 25
Jordan, David Starr, 3
Junior College Leadership Program,
126–27

K

Kellogg, W. K., Foundation, 126
Knoell, Dorothy, 10
Koos, Leonard V., 5

L

Lange, Alexis F., 5
Leadership programs, 126–27
at UCLA, 131
League for Innovation, 25
Los Angeles City College, 151–52

M

Marland, Sidney P., 10
Master teachers, inservice programs
for, 168
Masters' degree programs, 140
Matson, Jane, 24
Mayhew, Lewis, 99
Media aids, 70–71
Media specialists, 150
Minority-group students, 48–50
Multi-ethnic program coordinators, 93
Multimedia specialists, 95–96

N

National Center for Educational
Statistics, 80–81
National Defense Education Act, 129
National Faculty Association of
Community Junior Colleges, 143
Need for new community-junior
colleges, 2
Needs for development of staff, 115–19
New degree-granting programs, 140–53
Nonteaching staff *see* Staff
North Carolina State University,
129, 156–57

O

Occupational aspirations of students,
47–48
Occupational programs, 28–30
Open-door admission policies, 13–17
Orientation, faculty, 161–63

P

Packaged programs, 111–12
Paraprofessionals, 98–99, 149–53
Partnership Program, 148
"People's colleges," 10, 52